Land Contract Homes:

The Top 10 Mistakes
Home Buyer's Make...

And How to Avoid Them!

ᏮᏱᎦ

Michael Delaware

Published by
'If, And or But' Publishing Company
P.O. Box 2559
Battle Creek, Michigan 49016 USA
www.ifandorbutpublishing.com

ISBN-13: 978-0615956305
ISBN-10: 0615956300

This book also contains clipart illustrations which were acquired by means of royalty free usage rights in 2014 and are copyright to: *GraphicsFactory.com* on pages: Title Page, 1, 3, 7, 9, 11, 13-15, 35, 38, 43, 45, 53, 55, 63, 69, 75, 81, 84, 87, 88, 93, 99, 101, 109-111, 115-117, 121 & 129. All other illustrations are copyright to *If, And or But Publishing*.

While attempts have been made to verify all information provided in this publication; neither the author nor the publisher assumes any responsibility for errors, omissions, or contrary interpretations of the subject matter herein. The views expressed are those of the author alone, and should not be taken as expert instruction or commands. This book is sold with the understanding that neither the author nor the publisher is engaged in rendering legal, accounting, or other professional advice. If legal or other expert assistance is required, the services of a professional should be sought.

TABLE OF CONTENTS:

Introduction

❧❧

This book was prepared and compiled to help educate the reader on the subject of seller financing. A Land Contract, as will be explained in detail in this book is a form of seller financing wherein the buyer secures the home with a down payment, and makes monthly payments (inclusive of both interest and principle) to the seller over a period of time and stipulates that the buyer will settle the balance in full at a future date.

None of the information contained in this book is intended to constitute legal or other professional advice. You should not rely solely on the information contained in this book for making legal decisions. It is recommended one consult with an attorney or other professionals for specific advice tailored to your situation and for the area in which you are doing business.

The information contained herein has been obtained through sources deemed reliable but cannot be guaranteed as to its accuracy. Any information of special interest should be obtained through independent verification.

I use the term '*Land Contract*' as the main descriptive term for this type of seller financing throughout this book, as it is the most commonly known in the area of the Midwest U.S. where I reside. However, seller financing known as a 'Land Contract' is also commonly known as '*Contract for Deed*', '*Trust Deeds*', '*Deeds of Trust*', '*Notes*', '*Private Money Mortgages*', '*Privately Held Mortgages*' and '*Seller Financed Mortgages*' depending on the market or region you are in the country.

Some may have slight variations as to how they are executed within each State, but all essentially fall under the broad brushstroke description of 'Seller Financing'. For simplicity I use the term 'Land Contract' as the embracive term throughout this book. In this new edition of this book, I am also including an expanded resources page at the end where you may check out further information on this subject.

This book continues to expand on the subject of my first book '**Understanding Land Contract Homes: In Pursuit of the American Dream**' which was released in 2012. It helps to clarify key points that can create trouble for consumers venturing into a land contract arrangement without fully understanding the process.

The purpose of this new book (as well as with the previous ones I wrote on this subject) is to help the reader quickly identify the key areas that can create trouble with land contracts, as well as improve their understanding of the process.

This book will also help sellers who are seeking to sell residential property on land contact terms. It will cover the essential points of constructing an agreement, as well as the mistakes to avoid which can create future trouble down the road. If you have further interest in this subject as an investor, I have also written a companion book to this series entitled: **Land Contract Homes for Investors** which is available both in print and as an eBook.

Since the release of my first two books on this subject, I have received numerous calls from people from all over the country who were asking for help in sorting out a snarled up land contract agreement they had already entered upon. There were so many basic mistakes made, that sometimes I would spend hours on the phone backtracking to where they had to, so as to resolve the issue.

It occurred to me that it might be useful to write a new book covering not only the basics, but to address it from a point of view of targeting the major mistakes home buyers make. The 10 major mistakes are presented in this book. Of course there can be many, many mistakes people can make in any real estate process, but the ones listed here will definitely be the torpedo that can sink the whole deal if not avoided.

Many of the people I spoke to in the last few years were suffering from the effects of major legal situations because they had made one or more of the mistakes I define in this book. They not only lost a lot of money, but several of them lost the home they were intending to buy on land contract, and had to start over from scratch with nothing to show for it except a painful post disaster education.

So if you have read this far, and are still interested in land contracts, read on. Learn these 10 major mistakes, and more importantly, learn to avoid them. They are simple and easy to learn on the front end, and painful and expensive to learn after the fact.

6 ~ Land Contract Homes

What is a Land Contract?

❧

Land contracts are common throughout the United States. In some states, they are referred to as 'Trust Deeds', 'Contract for Deed', 'Deeds of Trust', 'Notes', 'Private Money Mortgages' or 'Privately Held Mortgages'. A "land contract" (sometimes referred to as an "installment sale agreement" or "contract for deed"), is a written contractual agreement between a seller and buyer of real estate in which the seller serves as the entity for financing, and the arrangement allows the buyer to acquire the property for an agreed-upon purchase price.

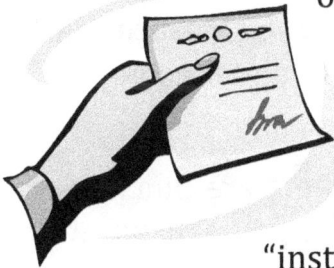

The buyer follows an installment payment structure to pay off the loan. There are variations in their structures, but essentially they consist of the basic concept of: *the seller is providing private financing to the buyer directly without involving a third party company.*

So, what is a 'Land Contract' or 'Contract for Deed' and how does it work?

For the purpose of this book, as established earlier, the term 'Land Contract' will be used to designate 'Seller Financing'. Keep in mind that the terms vary in different regions, as well as the method, but the underlying concept is the same: *Seller Financing.*

It is a seller held note, not backed by a conventional bank or financial institution, but by an individual or group under a land contract.

Within the agreement there are timelines established, due dates for payments as well as a defined time when the contract must be paid off in full through either a lump sum cash payment (often called a *'Balloon'* payment) or a settlement through means refinancing with another loan.

Regardless of the name used, they essentially represent the same concept: a method of selling property where the buyer 'borrows' from or relies upon the seller for the financing rather than paying cash up front or obtaining a direct loan from a bank.

The seller throughout the contract all the way to the end holds the legal title to the property. The buyer is permitted to take possession of the home for all defined purposes, but does do not gain final legal ownership until the loan is paid in full, much like a conventional mortgage.

The buyer has ownership *rights*, and is responsible for payment of taxes, insurance and maintaining the property just as with any written agreement with a mortgage company. *Rights of ownership* could best be defined as: *the ability to control the outcome of purchase, sale or improvements to a property one possesses.*

Rights also include the right to control what is being built or what the property is used for and the right to exclude other people from entering the owned property. A property owner must have a deed or title to the property in order to enjoy the rights afforded by property ownership and may be forced to prove ownership in court.

The buyer's ownership rights are subject to the conditions of a land contract being in effect, the payments not being in default and all payments being made. In some cases, an escrow account may be set up between the seller and buyer maintained by a third party to collect monthly contributions toward the payment of taxes, insurance and any property-related fees to be disbursed annually or semi-annually when the bills come due.

The agreed-upon purchase price of the sale is commonly paid over time in periodic installment payments. This frequently includes a balloon payment at some future time period defined to make the time length of payments shorter than a customary commercial loan, which usually has no final balloon payment.

Commonly, the balloon payments are made within a set time frame within the land contract agreement to be reached in two to five years, depending on the amount of the loan, but can be as long as ten years. This is a negotiable point between both parties, and can be set shorter or longer depending on the situation.

When the agreed upon purchase price has been paid inclusive of any interest, the seller is then required to transfer legal title of the property to the buyer.

This is where it becomes important for a land contract to be recorded with the property registry of deeds in the area to maintain property rights for the buyer, and seller through the course of this transaction. This will be discussed further in a later chapter.

A down payment based on a percentage of the agreed upon sales price is usually required from the buyer to initiate a land contract, paid to the seller as the first major payment on the property so as to secure the buyers ownership interests (*rights*).

The legal status of land contracts varies from state to state, and region to region. State laws should be reviewed in any situation where parties are considering such an agreement.

Understanding Land Contract Key Components

⥀⥁

The earliest forms of contracts were in the form of '*verbal agreements*'. In fact, verbal contract still exist today. You maybe even made one today if you ate at a restaurant.

Now, you might be thinking "Really? What contract did I make there? I just ate some food!" However, even ordering food at a restaurant involves a contract of sorts.

Essentially whenever you order food at a restaurant, you enter into a verbal agreement that implies that they will serve you the food of your choice, and you agree to pay the bill for that food and service before you leave. That is a basic example of a verbal contract. A service is exchanged, or a product, or both, usually over a short period of time.

If someone were to engage in a verbal contract on the purchase of land, for example, they could verbally agree on a price and then a monthly payment. However, if the verbal agreement goes on too long, one side might claim they forgot and decide not to fulfill the agreement, or change their mind, etc.

Also, consider what can happen to a verbal contract if one of the people agreeing to the terms dies, or has an accident that leaves them incapable of fulfilling the agreement? Many circumstances or changes can occur over time that makes a verbal contract unstable for use over a long period of time.

So with that we can see that a written agreement become necessary the longer or larger a transaction becomes. The moment 'Time' is entered into an agreement, it becomes necessary to put things into written form to encompass the broad range of variables and unpredictable circumstances that can happen over time. Even with a written agreement, one must think in terms of the future in hopes to cover all possible eventualities.

Imagine for a moment the 'Wild West'. Two people want to transact business on a piece of land, and work out a written agreement with payments they both agree to initially. As problems come along, both learn from the experience, and either hire another person to help them (usually an attorney) to help them look at the arrangement to see how they could re-write it to define what should happen in certain circumstances. Or they could do a shoot-out.

Does a contract survive death? Suppose one of the two parties dies before the land contract is completed? What then? Let's assume they finished this initial agreement and then later wanted to transact business on a piece of land again, but this time there is a house on it. Consider this for a moment, as this introduces a lot of new variables.

What happens if someone does not pay, can they be removed? What happens if they do not want to go? What happens if the place burns down, is stampeded with cattle or washed away in a flood? What if the married couple who live there get divorced, and one kicks the other out and the other refuses to pay for the home, and the one remaining in it cannot?

Imagine all of these scenarios. These variables may become components of a contract because somewhere along the line that may happened here to someone. It became necessary to have these rules written into the agreement so that everyone understands the rules before going into the agreement.

So let's look at some of the key components of a land contract from that perspective for a moment. There are several key components of a basic Land Contract. Every State in the U.S. will have variations on these, as well as additional components not listed here. The following chapter is provided to give the reader a starting point for some of the common components found in this type of sellers financing agreement.

Some of the key components of a Land Contract are defined in the following sections:

People Involved in the Contract

The "Parties" in the contract are the 'people' involved in the transaction, and includes the full legal names of the individuals (and their addresses) that are entering into the contract. It is recommended that the names match the exact legal identifications, such as a driver's license. This would include the middle initials and middle names where applicable. Avoid the use of nicknames in a legal document.

A party can also be another entity such as a: Limited Liability Company, Corporation, Non-Profit, Partnership or some other legal group entity. In such a case, the contract will reference the documents that establish this legal entity, such as: *corporate papers, articles of organization, etc.*

The "Seller" is the person who is selling the property and is usually listed first. The "Purchaser" is the one purchasing (buying) the property and is usually listed in sequence after the Seller on the documents.

Legal Description

When a seller is agreeing to sell vacant land, residential or some other form of commercial property, the Seller is agreeing in the contract to convey (sell) to the Purchaser a very specifically described parcel of land. This description must be exact. When the purchase is completed and paid off, this should match the description on the deed. The city, village, or township of the property is noted, as well as county and state.

Using the mailing address of the property is not enough. The mailing address of a property is designed for use by the postal service, and is not the legal description. There are several types of legal descriptions on property. Some define the location on the County parcels, including the city, township, village, etc. and down to the section of the grid and parcel number. Inner city properties will commonly have a shorter description defining a parcel and lot number.

Here is an example of what one of these looks like:

'Highland Hills Park E 1/2 Of Lot 51, All Of Lot 52'

Others describe it from a stake survey marking a point of beginning, and measuring out the boundaries of the defined land. These are common in rural properties.

Here is an example of one of these looks like:

'Athens Twp/T4s R8w, Sec. 22: Beg At Pt N24deg 25'e 641.24 Ft From A Pt 1631.7 Ft E Of W 1/4 Pst On E & W 1/4 Ln Of Sec., Th S24deg 25'w 96 Ft. N65deg 31'w 265 Ft M/L To Ctr Ln Of Hwy Ne'ly Alng Sd CtR Ln 95 Ft S65deg 35'e 265 Ft M/Lto P.O.B. (Sub To R.O.W. In The Nw'ly 100 Ft Thereof).'

This last one is called a 'Metes and Bounds' legal description. One does not need to become a surveyor to understand this subject, as long as they make sure that the legal description on the contract matches what is on the deed. You can see from this example that they can be comprehensive, so it is vital that it conforms exactly to the property being sold.

As the purchase includes not only the soil, vegetation, trees, water, etc. throughout the parameters defined in the legal description, the Seller also conveys such things as any buildings, easements, tenements, improvements and appurtenances.

Buildings: Any structure on the land, including the house, garage, sheds, pole barns, etc.

Easements: A right to cross over access or otherwise use someone else's land for a specified purpose. This can be shared driveway between two adjoining homes, for example.

Tenements: Any room or rooms forming a separate residence within a block of apartments or house.

Improvements: Any structures on the property or additions to the property that add value, such as trees or a swimming pool for example.

Appurtenances: Pertaining to something that attaches. In real estate law this describes any restriction or right which goes with a property, such as an easement to gain access across the neighbor's parcel. Another example might be a covenant (agreement) against blocking the neighbor's view.

In short, the Seller conveys everything that is permanently affixed to the property, as well as all the above rights and restrictions as applicable. A good way to look at this is as anything screwed, bolted, glued or nailed down as remaining with the home as a 'fixture'. This will include any structures on the land as well.

Anything that can be detached with a simple plug or hook, wheeled off or un-hung from a nail are non-fixtures. This can include appliances, and will depend as to whether they are affixed or not based on the above description. For example: a dishwasher is often regarded as a fixture, as it is plumbed, screwed or bolted in, whereas a refrigerator is not, as it is simply plugged in.

Price and Terms of Payment

This area should contain all the numerical values concerning sales price, costs and also timeframes in terms of dates:

The date of the Contract is here at the beginning as well. Interest starts to "accrue" (begins being owed to the Seller) starting from the date typed in, at the top of the contract. Consequently, when the first payment is due, one month's interest is usually already owed, since it is customarily paid in arrears (paying at the end of a period of which it is incurred).

The 'numerical values' will include such things as the final purchase price and the dollar value of down payment. It will also include the beginning balance in the contract (this is calculated as the purchase price minus the dollar value of the down payment). It will also establish the monthly payment (or in some cases the annual or semi-annual payment), what the agreed upon interest rate is (this is commonly defined in terms of an annual rate).

The contract will further define when the date of the 'balloon' payment (if any) shall fall, and a specific date that the first payment is due, along with which day of the month future payments will be due throughout the contract. A 'balloon payment' is essentially a point defined in the future where the entire note becomes due.

Purchase Price - The 'agreed upon Purchase price' (sometimes defined legally as "consideration") is negotiated between the Seller and the Purchaser. Properties sold on a land contract commonly are sold for more in terms of sale value in the agreed upon purchase price than properties that are sold for cash simply because the Seller is providing the financing, which is what is considered all-important to the buyer. If the seller has another note the purchase price should be higher than the balance owed.

Down Payment - The down payment is customarily 10% to 20% of the agreed upon purchase price. It represents funds that the seller does not have to collect in the process of the purchase, and it also represents the Purchaser's commitment to buying the property. Sometimes, non-cash down payments (barter items such as used cars, boats, tractors, snowmobiles, applied rent, other property, etc.) can be used as a form of a down payment (full or in part). There can be very creative ways to structure a sale. These options are not readily available through a conventional lending institution. This is a distinct advantage of a Land Contract.

Balance Remaining - This defines the amount that is the purchase price subtracting the numerical value of the down payment. The balance remaining will decrease each month

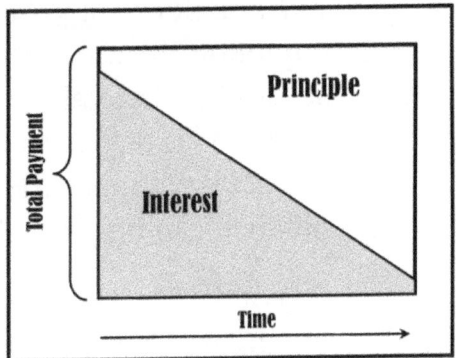

with every payment made by the new home owner. An 'amortization schedule' shows how the balance will be reduced if monthly payments are made on time. An 'amortization schedule' is best defined as: "complete schedules of loan payments, showing the amount of principal and the amount of interest that comprise each payment". Often the agreement references the amortization schedule which is usually a printed attachment to the finalized Land Contract.

Monthly Payment - The monthly payment formula is most commonly about 1% to 1.5% of the beginning or starting balance was defined on the contract. If after the down payment the Seller is owed $50,000 by the Purchaser, the monthly payment will probably be in the neighborhood of $500 to $750.

The smaller in size of the monthly payment, the longer in time it will take to settle the final value or remaining balance owed in land contract and the larger the monthly payment the faster the remaining balance can be paid off.

Payment Due Date - It is the date defined for the initial payment being due and also refers to the specific day of the month each consecutive payment agreed to be due. This date is a negotiable point between buyer and seller. Failing to make payment on a due date could also result in late fees, and these will also be defined in the agreement.

Grace Period - In some contracts, a grace period is defined. This allows the Purchaser a few days each month during which payments are due and not be considered in default. Some contracts will establish a late fee in the agreement if the payment is not received by the defined time or within the timeframe established as the 'grace period'. Grace periods and/or late fee clauses are customarily included at the end of the contract as miscellaneous provisions, but are none the less important to note.

Home buyers can commonly mistake the last day of the grace period as the payment due date. It must be realized that even though a late fee is not being charged, the payment is still late in terms of contract performance. Although a Land Contract holder is not likely to report to a credit agency, they might. Also, if you ever need a good reference on your performance, pay on time and always before the grace period.

Balloon Payment - A balloon payment is the term used for a final lump sum payment on the contract. Balloon clauses usually call for the final payment to be made on a specified date. A contract may contain a clause that reads something like, "the entire purchase price plus defined interest shall be paid in full within three years from the date hereof, anything herein to the contrary notwithstanding". This is what is referred to as a 'balloon' in the contract (a three year balloon, in this example).

If the Purchaser fails to make a balloon payment when required, this most often will constitute a default on the contract, unless some other provision is made. It is common to see a balloon payment defined as either: 2, 3, 5 or even 10 years depending on what is negotiated. A balloon payment can define that the remaining balance be simply paid minus interest, or plus interest, so this is important to note.

Defined Interest Rate - The interest rate is a percentage rate commonly defined as an annual term, (e.g., 9%, 11%, etc). When

one records each payment made, interest is
then calculated for the payment period
(usually monthly) by multiplying the
interest rate by the remaining balance due.
It is then calculated each consecutive
payment as the annual interest amount by
the number of payments to be made each
year.

Here is an example as reflected on an
amortization schedule with an 11% interest
rate on a loan of $100,000 over a15 year
period, with the first 12 payments
represented here:

Month	Payment	Interest	Principle	Balance
1	$1,136.00	$916.67	$219.93	$99,780.07
2	$1,136.00	$914.67	$221.95	$99,558.12
3	$1,136.00	$912.62	$223.98	$99,334.14
4	$1,136.00	$910.56	$226.04	$99,108.10
5	$1,136.00	$908.49	$228.11	$98,879.99
6	$1,136.00	$906.40	$230.20	$98,649.79
7	$1,136.00	$904.29	$232.31	$98,417.48
8	$1,136.00	$902.16	$234.44	$98,183.04
9	$1,136.00	$900.01	$236.59	$97,946.45
10	$1,136.00	$897.84	$238.76	$97,707.69
11	$1,136.00	$895.65	$240.95	$97,466.74
12	$1,136.00	$893.45	$243.15	$97,223.59

This calculated value which it the total
interest for the period, is subsequently
deducted from the payment as shown in the
example above. The rest of the payment is

known as the 'principal' portion of the payment and is then subtracted from the adjusted remaining principal balance as the balance is reduced following the terms of the contract.

As an additional note on this, it is common for uninformed buyers to take issue with a higher interest rate that a seller is offering, which exceeds perhaps a local loan rate.

There really is no exact correlation between interest rates on a loan offered by a bank or credit union and interest rates on a Land Contract.

Land Contracts are typically higher, as you are working with a private seller. It should be understood, however, that the seller, lacking the resources of a large lender, assumes more of a risk in offering financing.

Typically this risk is compensated with a higher interest rate, a larger down payment or both.

Taxes and Insurance

The party who becomes responsible for paying the tax and insurance payments on the property depends upon what is defined in the terms of the land contract. Property taxes can be in the form of a singular payment, or divided into separate bills for State, County, Township or Village, depending on the practices followed in your area.

Check with your local Assessor's office for details on this. Insurance typically is just a homeowner's coverage. However in certain areas of the country flood insurance or 'Wind' insurance may be an additional requirement.

The three common methods to structure the taxes and insurance payments on the property, and define who is responsible for this and what method will be used are as follows:

> The Purchaser pays the required taxes and insurance; or

> The Seller pays the required taxes and insurance and then adds the exact value of amounts paid back to the balance on the contract; or

> The Purchaser makes monthly payments to an escrow account held by the Seller and the Seller pays the required taxes and insurance premiums out of this account.

Method 1: Purchaser pays the Taxes and Insurance premiums

Customarily the most common of these methods is that the Purchaser is the party responsible for paying the taxes and insurance premiums on the property. A typical clause in a land contract where the Purchaser pays the property taxes and insurance premiums is often written as this:

"The Purchaser agrees to pay all assessments and taxes hereafter levied on said premises ..."

Method 2: Seller pays and re-adds the amount spent back amount spent to contract principle balance.

Since failure to pay either the tax or the insurance bills can seriously place at risk the value of the property and investment defined in the land contract (imagine trying to collect payments on an uninsured home that was destroyed in a flood, destroyed in a storm or was lost in a fire!).

For this reason, some Sellers demand to pay the property tax and insurance premiums themselves. After making payments on these bills, the Sellers just add the expenses of insurance and taxes back onto the end balance of the land contract at the time that the tax payments and insurance premiums are paid, and then send a statement to the buyer.

These statements can be monthly, quarterly or annually as defined in the agreement. Contracts of this type are sometimes referred to as 'Back Loaded' or in some cases referred to as amounts 'Added Back'. This may be a viable option if a seller lives out of State, and wants reassurance that these are paid. It can also be a good option for someone who lacks the time, ability or resources to verify the payments are made, as when one is selling the home for an elder parent in a nursing home, for example.

When using this option, the monthly payment will commonly be increased with an estimated amount to cover the approximated one-twelfth of the estimated taxes along with the required premiums for insurance. These payments are treated just as if the entire amount of each payment was for principal and interest, with the added larger value to cover the estimated one-twelfth fee for the property taxes and insurance.

This can make the balance on the contract drop at a more rapid rate that it customarily would. However, one must also factor in that when the tax and insurance bills are delivered to the Seller, the Seller remits payment to them and then adds the value of the funds spent to the end balance due on the land contract.

Therefore, the final remaining balance on the land contract, after having been reduced each month more than it normally would be due to the larger payments, is then re-adjusted upward when the amounts for property taxes and insurance premiums are added back to the contract balance.

Method 3: Seller Pays Taxes and Insurance out of Amounts Put in Escrow

A third method to address how the property taxes and insurance premiums are paid is similar to Method 2. In this method the Purchaser pay approximately one-twelfth of the estimated property taxes and insurance premiums in addition to each monthly payment installment. The Seller places these added funds into a special account each month, in what is called an "escrow account" to remit payment for these bills as they are due.

If the escrow account ever becomes insufficient to pay these bills, the Seller notifies the Purchaser and a new adjusted higher value of the escrow payment is then required to be included along with the next monthly payment. Terms and compliance for this is defined in the contract. Commonly, adjustments are made annually when using this method.

Sometimes escrow accounts can be maintained by using a separate entity. Some banks or Title companies might offer this service in your area. In any event, there are precise accounting procedures that must be followed with escrow accounts, and it is recommended that you consult with a Certified Public Accountant regarding the laws pertaining to your State.

Seller's Right to Mortgage

The Seller has the right to borrow against his or her remaining equity in the property sold. In other words, if the Seller owned a $50,000 property free and clear and then sold it to the Purchaser with a $10,000 down payment, the Seller initially has the right to collect $40,000 (his or her remaining equity in the property) and he or she may borrow money by allowing a lender to put a senior lien on the property (ahead of the Purchaser's interest in the property) for up to $40,000.

However, since the Seller must be in a position at all times to convey the Deed to the property when the Purchaser makes the final payment on the contract, the Seller can never owe more on the property than he or she is owed by the Purchaser.

To protect the Purchaser from any debts that the Seller may have against the property, the Seller must provide notice of any such mortgage and its terms in a certified letter to the Purchaser.

The Purchaser also has the right to make the payments for the Seller on any debt for which the Seller is in default. Any such payment made by the Purchaser, of course, will be deducted from the monthly payment owed by the Purchaser to the Seller.

As an example: *If a home one is buying receives a foreclosure notice from the original lender, one has a right to pay that payment directly to prevent default of one chooses.*

To summarize, the Seller must never owe on the property more than he or she is owed. To engage in such an agreement otherwise is to make for an inequitable transaction, and invite future complications which could have legal ramifications.

Purchaser's Duties to Maintain Premises

It is the Purchaser's duty to protect and maintain the value of the property he or she is buying until the final balance on the land contract is settled in full. Therefore a clause defining this duty is included in most contracts, and it is important because it is the value of the property that keeps the Purchaser making payments.

Should the Purchaser ever go into default and be required to return the home to the seller by means of forfeiture or foreclosure, it is this retained value of the condition of the property that enables a Seller to re-sell it without a loss.

Most land contracts require the Purchaser to notify the Seller in writing before the Purchaser or any third party alters or demolishes any buildings, commits waste (neglects or damages the property or allows it to be used in a way that would lessen resale value) or removes and/or makes improvements on the premises in a way which may lesson, alter or ultimately diminish the property's value in terms of resale.

The contract may stipulate that one cannot dispose of hazardous waste on the property either, such as disposing of oil, fuel, industrial waste, radioactive material, etc. Disposing of such chemicals can affect ground water, and well systems, and can greatly reduce the value of a property to say the least. Abandonment of old vehicles and violations of city ordinances concerning property condition could also fall into this category, for example.

Seller's Duty to Provide Proof of Title and Convey (or 'Deed over') Premises

Once the buyer has made the final payment on the land contract without default, the Seller is required to convey the property by signing over a Deed to the exact property defined in the legal description as the property.

Upon delivering the Deed, the Seller often additionally delivers an 'abstract of title' (A shortened or condensed history, taken from public records or documents, of the ownership of a piece of land, most often prepared by an attorney) or a policy of title insurance demonstrating that the property is free and clear from any liens that the Seller may have remaining or had in prior history on the property.

The party that is required to cover the expense of the insurance should be agreed upon when the land contract is initiated.

It is recommended for the protection of both parties that they obtain title insurance on the property being sold, before they enter into a Land Contract agreement.

It is particularly important for the buyer to verify the seller is indeed the rightful owner of the property. More on this will be covered in a later chapter concerning prevention of fraud.

It is the Purchaser's responsibility to record the Deed. The fee is nominal and recording the Deed will show as a matter of public record that the Purchaser is the new owner of the property.

Assignment of the Contract

A seller commonly wants to retain the right to freely assign his or her interest in the land contract to another party. This means that a seller can sell the Land Contract to another investor if they choose. (An exception might be if the Seller is still making payments on the property themselves and the original contract governing that purchase restricts or prevents the Seller's from being able to assign.)

The Purchaser in a land contract often has the right to assign his or her interest in the contract; however it is most commonly restricted to 'only after obtaining written permission from the Seller'. Essentially, one cannot have someone else take over the responsibility of the Land Contract payments and absolve oneself from any liability in the event of future default.

This clause protects the Seller. It exists simply due to the fact that a Seller may only have sold the property to the buyer on the strength of the Purchaser's credit rating, employment stability, or character, along with other factors.

When this Purchaser then proposes to change to a new party, who will then become the primarily responsible person for performing on payments to the Seller in a land contract, the Seller is entitled to and given the right to review, makes examination and evaluate this new purchaser and approve such a change to the original agreement in writing.

Further, any approved assignment by the Purchaser to this new purchaser quite often does not release the original Purchaser from the obligation to perform under the contract should the new purchaser default on the original land contract.

Default

If the Purchaser fails to make payment or perform any significant part of the contract it is then considered to be in 'default'. The Seller quite often has the right, after notifying the Purchaser in writing of the exact nature of the default, to regard all previous payments made to the date of the default on the contract as simply 'rental payments' made by the Purchaser. State laws vary on this point from State to State. Some jurisdictions have specific guidelines regarding default on land contracts, so be sure to check with legal professionals.

If the default continues, the Seller has the right to declare the remaining balance due and payable, and if the default is not then cleared up or the contract is not paid in full, the Seller can begin steps to regain possession of the property. Improvements made to the property by the Purchaser then become the Seller's property.

Most often default by the Purchaser is commonly a failure to make timely payments. However, default can also include failure to pay insurance premiums and therefore adequately insure the property, failure to pay property taxes as they become due or failure to properly safeguard against damage and waste or maintain the value property. See later chapter on remedies for default.

Miscellaneous Provisions

Most all contracts close with a list or section of detailed 'miscellaneous provisions' regarding where the notices and payments should be mailed, which state law is governing the specific agreement, and so forth. The common provisions in a basic or standard pre-printed land contract are secondary to importance of typed provisions at the end of a negotiated contract, as these represent the unique terms negotiated between buyer and seller. Be certain to read, interpret and enforce these typed provisions carefully.

Signatures and Notarization

In order for a Land Contract to be recorded in the local county records in the area that the property is located, you are required to have the contract notarized by a licensed notary.

This does not necessarily require a notary from that State, but their license must be in force and current. There is usually no fee for this service, and if there is a fee, it is usually nominal. Some states prohibit a notary from charging a fee.

Witnesses will often be needed as signatory in the contract, and they will need to be available to observe the signing of the contract when it happens. This may also be done in front of a notary.

It is further recommended that identification of all parties, including the witnesses be obtained for the records. This is particularly important for the seller. This verification of identification for the records can be a copy of their driver's license or passport, for example. Most attorney offices and title companies require this now as part of the Homeland Security Regulations.

Summary

Keeping in mind these key components, let's go through the top 10 major mistakes consumers make, and discuss how to avoid them one by one...

MISTAKE #1: A GENERAL LACK OF UNDERSTANDING ON LAND CONTRACTS

જ્જ્જ્જ

It may seem obvious that if you engage in a legal arrangement with someone and do not understand what arrangement you are getting into (much less one's responsibilities in the matter) that one could wind up in trouble. As simple as this may sound, the court rooms are filled with people suing people over contracts they entered into and did not fully understand the agreements that they were signing.

Let's back up a step and explore what occurs just before things go awry. For example, someone enters into an agreement to rent an apartment and then moves in and finds out that every morning the trains go by and shake the whole building. Or someone buys an automobile, and drives it off the lot only to have the transmission fall out as one gets onto the highway. The buyer is blinded by the pursuit of something they wanted so strongly that they omitted to really look. They may have skipped the step of standing back and inspecting what they were buying, making inquiries from others who have bought this item or service, or involving an expert to help them with aspects of the transaction they were not in familiar territory with.

In the previous example, the prospective apartment renter could have inquired with neighbors independently and asked them how they like living there, and might have discovered the noisy train issue before signing the lease.

They could have also brought in an expert familiar with the area and have them look it over for them to see if they noticed anything or could offer insight into anything they were not seeing.

Instead, they visited the apartment and were given a tour by a representative of the complex and got caught up in the glow of having their own apartment and the result was disappointment.

In the other example of the car buyer who bought a car with the bad transmission, perhaps they elected to do a short test drive and take all the dealerships information as fact and did not question it. Perhaps they did not bring in an outside expert who was familiar with that type of car to have them look it over and give them their opinion. They like the apartment hunter probably purchased the car driven by the blind desire to own the car because it was something they fancied. It looked cool! It was sporty or the right color!

Both of these buyers skipped an important step: *Becoming educated on the process instead of being driven by the passion of the outcome.*

During the times I have encountered people who had a snarled up legal situations with a land contract agreement it always started where they were so excited to be able to buy a house after being turned down by a bank that they were willing to sign almost anything when given the opportunity.

Some deliberately did not involve professionals to review the agreement for fear that they would try to talk them out of it. They blindly entered into the land contract with the idea they could fix anything if something were to go wrong down the road.

As a result most walked into situations that in fact could not be resolved later on.

Here are a few examples:

Example #1: The undisclosed mortgage

One family purchased a home on land contract and discovered later that the owner who sold it to them had never disclosed to them that there was a mortgage on the property.

The sellers took their down payment, and collected monthly payments for two years before allowing the home to go into foreclosure.

The family not only lost the home because the mortgage company foreclosed, they lost all of their investment which totaled over ten thousand dollars. Additionally they had invested another five thousand dollars into remodeling the bathroom, and that of course was lost too when the home was taken in foreclosure.

Example #2: The fake owner

Another example I encountered was when a buyer purchased a home on land contract and after three months of making payments discovered that the person who sold it to them was not the owner of the home and the original owners were simply out of town living in a nursing home and their family had asked an acquaintance of one of the siblings who supposedly 'knew something about houses' to look after it for them.

The family 'friend' sold the home to buyers who did not pay for title insurance and he skipped town with their down payment, and three months of payments before getting a notice from the sheriff to vacate as squatters.

Example #3: The wrong owner

One woman called me who had made payments to a man for three years on a land contract home, and later the man got divorced and the buyer learned that the man was not the legal owner of the property. The legal owner was his soon to be ex-wife's mother, and the rest of the family thought he was renting it to buyers. Instead he took their down payment and spent it without telling his wife.

The whole house of cards collapsed when the divorce proceedings started and the buyers learned they had no legal ownership of the property. The buyers had previously looked at public records, and the name on the deed appeared to match the man's wife's name so they signed the agreement. Had they paid for title work, they would have learned that the man's wife had the same name as her mother only with a different spelling of the first name.

Essentially what one can learn from the above three examples is that it pays to pause for a moment and do some homework. There can be many issues that can come up with regards to having a clear title to the property you are buying. There can be many points of a contract that you need to understand the ramifications of for failure to perform by either party. One also must know the various ways to protect and safeguard your investment by making sure the home is insured and the taxes are paid.

I will go into more details about this in the following chapters. Don't get caught up in the glow of excitement of having found a place to live and raise your family at an affordable rate and neglect to really look at the business side of the transaction and recognize how you are investing your money.

Land Contracts, like any form of purchasing or acquiring real estate is a form of investment. Taking the correct steps to protect your investment makes for a happy future. Skipping or omitting vital steps to secure your rights to the property can mean you are on the losing side of a bad investment.

In today's economy no one wants to lose out and start over again after years of commitment to an investment in real estate. Take a deep breath, understand the process.

The process of land contracts is explained in my previous book entitled: '*Understanding Land Contract Homes: In Pursuit of the American Dream*'. There is also more information available in my other book entitled: '*Land Contract Homes for Investors*'. Those two books along with the information presented in the following chapters of this book will go a long way to make you a well educated buyer.

Other ways to become informed are to consult professionals. Consider having any deal reviewed by an attorney, Title Company or your Realtor.

Make sure you understand fully any agreement you are signing. Don't commit to an agreement you do not fully understand.

In the purchase of any home there is a consideration about three things: *Past, Present* and *Future*. Examining these individually can help you better understand the property.

The Past

Learn as much as you can about the past history of the home through inspections, speaking with neighbors or checking with public tax or assessment records. Also take some time to check out the person you are buying from. Check with public records at the court house and find out if there are any pending lawsuits on this person concerning real estate transactions. Make sure there is no past pattern of behavior that could raise a red flag to the business relationship you are about to engage in.

The Present

Really look at the home in its present condition. Have it inspected and find out if it needs vital repairs now. Make sure you study the contract you are being asked to sign in present time and be sure you understand what you are agreeing to.

Look at what you see, not what you are being told. Investigate with the local police department on the crime rate in the area. Check current tax and assessors records for liens. Check with the courts for pending litigation concerning the owner or this property. Use a title company to verify the seller has a clean title.

The Future

Make sure you understand what the future commitments will be on your part regarding this transaction. Whose responsibility is it to verify taxes and insurance are paid? When will the balloon payment come due? What financial position will you need to be in down the road to refinance the house or settle a balloon payment? There are many points within the contract itself that address the future. Be certain that you understand those, or consult with a professional who can help you with this.

Summary

To summarize this chapter, there are three key points to consider in this:

> ➤ Educate yourself on the process and understand how land contracts work. Read books, and most importantly, read and understand the contract you are being asked to sign.

> ➤ Consult with professionals who work for you, not for someone else. Ask for

their help in reviewing the contract, inspecting the home, or answering basic questions to increase your understanding of the home and the contract you are going to commit to.

➢ Recognize there is a past, present and future with any real estate and its transaction. Take steps to understand each independently.

MISTAKE #2: FAILING TO VERIFY OWNERSHIP

ॐॐ

What does ownership mean? Ownership is defined as: 'the act, state, or right of possessing something'. In a legal sense it is: *the legal right of possession; proprietorship*. It is a quality of a right of possession. In regards to sole ownership and this right of possession, one can dictate what can be done with this possession without having to consult anyone else, as no one else has rights to do so.

When one discusses 'Property rights' one is referring to: *the legal right of ownership of a property*. The person who possesses the rights of ownership can retain this property as long as they wish, and also retain the legal ability to transfer ownership of the property to another or others.

In short, a person who has legal ownership of a property can transfer ownership to another. They can deed a home over to someone and release their rights with or without money changing hands if they so wish, although in some States it is required to record a sales price even if it is just 1$ as one might be gifting a home over to a relative. A property can be owned by more than one person, a group of people, or another legal entity.

When it comes to land contracts one of the biggest mistakes one can make is to engage in a land contract with a seller without verifying their legal ownership of the home, and, thus, have the exclusive rights to sell it to you. Skipping the step of verifying ownership through independent research can result in an expensive legal situation down the road.

Here are some real life case examples I have encountered over the years to illustrate this point:

Case #1: The Con Artist

I worked with a woman once in selling some properties she owned. She had gotten involved with a man who represented himself as a real estate investor and businessman who could help her purchase investment homes and manage them for her. He convinced her that all she needed to do was purchase the home, and he would take care of the rest including collecting the rents, paying the taxes, insurance and mortgage payments. She would simply get a profit check in her mailbox every month to spend as she wished.

She did not consult with any other professionals to see if this was a safe investment. She did not do a background check on the man to find out if there were any pending legal situations regarding him to raise a red flag, nor did she ask for references. She simply bought into his reassuring and convincing personality, and got caught up in the glow of the prospect of a monthly profit check coming to her in her mailbox.

She purchased five houses with her good credit and turned control over to him after purchase. In the beginning she received profit checks in the mail each month, and so settled back with the idea she had made wise decisions with her money.

What she discovered later was that she had a total legal disaster on her hands. The man had rented one of the homes, and sold the other four on land contracts to prospective buyers. He took a sizeable down payment from each buyer and pocketed it. He pocketed all of the taxes and insurance escrow money as well. He sent her a rent check each month from the one house and pocketed the rest. He made about three mortgage payments on each home and then let them all quietly go into default after he transferred all the mail to his own address.

He was able to hide all of the foreclosures from her for a time, until one day when she happened to receive a notice in her own mail on one of the mortgages. By that time the damage was irreparable. She was in default by several months on all five homes and two had already been sold on the courthouse steps and were in the redemption period for which her only option was to pay off the note in full or let it go.

The four buyers on land contracts on the homes lost their investments in full. One had spent considerable money remodeling his new home, and all of that investment was lost as well when the home was sold at foreclosure and the families occupying the homes were evicted.

When she finally approached me as a Realtor to help her sort it out, all we could do was try to sell the homes before they were lost to foreclosure and essentially do damage control on her credit by settling some of the debt. I managed to sell two of the homes for her. The others were so badly damaged by the former occupants who retaliated against the property when they learned about their pending loss.

I also contacted the FBI and connected her with the local field agent there and he took all of her information and began an investigation on this man. Whether he was ever prosecuted I do not know. He had done this same scheme with four other women, and I helped some of them sell off their homes as well.

Case #2: The Divorce Entanglement

I spoke with one buyer who called me after my first book came out. She explained to me that she and her husband had purchased a home on land contract from a man and had made payments for a period of about three years. They had originally put down five thousand dollars as the down payment.

She had contacted the man with a desire to refinance and settle the note. He refused to meet with her and became confrontational with her on the phone. She finally went to an attorney to seek help and discovered that the man did not own the property exclusively, and that he co-owned it with his wife. The couple was mid a divorce, and the man never told his wife that he had sold the home on land contract. Further investigation revealed that the couple did not have a clear title to the home, as there were several contractor liens on the property as well.

The buyer who had spent three years investing in the home with her children happily in school and had friends in the neighborhood, etc. was not facing the fact that she could lose her home as the seller did not have clear title nor the exclusive right to sell the home to her and her husband. Making matters worse the ownership rights were now entangled in the couple's divorce situation and sorting it out was going to require extensive legal work.

Case #3: I'll sell to you, but don't involve a Realtor...

I spoke with a man who called me after seeing my books online and reading one of my blog articles on land contracts. He said that he purchased a home from a man about three months prior on land contract. The seller told him that he would sell the home to him, as long as he did not involve a Realtor. When he inquired as to why this was, the man said something about not wanting to 'complicate' things or 'pay Realtor fees' etc. He agreed to the deal.

Within three months after he purchased the home, a notice arrived at his house from the assessor's office regarding an unpaid municipal assessment. It also mentioned another person's name other than his or the prior owner. At that point he decided to call a Realtor and ask for help.

He found out from a local Realtor after a little investigation in public records that the home was deeded in the name of another party, and not the prior seller or himself.

Additionally there was an unpaid municipal assessment on the property, as well as back taxes owed. Further investigation revealed that the city had the home on the condemned list, and the occupancy permit had been revoked and the buyer was not legally permitted to occupy the residence. His inquiries into the matter with the city triggered a legal *order to vacate* which was mailed to him by the abandoned buildings department.

Had the prospective buyer involved a professional such as a Realtor, attorney or Title Agency many of these red flags would likely have been found before he made a commitment. Instead the buyer being new to real estate purchases took the exclusive *'I'm your friend with the old school hand-shake sales pitch'* and he sailed right into a messy real estate entanglement.

How do you verify ownership of a property?

Most of this information is available in public records. Verifying ownership requires that you go to the register of deeds or County Assessor's office and obtain copies of what is recorded in public records as to who legally owns the property. In doing so, one will also be able to find out if there are any recorded mortgages, liens on the property or any other recorded instrument affecting ownership of the property.

Checking with the local tax assessor can let you know if there are back taxes owed. Any sale of a home should require the seller pay any back taxes in full as part of the agreement.

The average buyer may not be comfortable with taking the time to do this. There are companies that can help you with this. That type of company is called a *Title Company* (or in some States it is an *Abstract Attorney*). Hiring them for a fee can help you with a title search of ownership on the home to verify who the legal owner is, and who has rights to sell the home to you. They can also uncover many other defect or errors in the history of title of the property.

Ownership by Other Legal Entities

Sometimes a home is owned by a legal entity other than an individual. It can be owned by a corporation or a Limited Liability Company (LLC). In determining whether a person has the legal right to sell you the home, you should request a copy of the corporate memorandum that authorizes the person selling you the home the legal authority to do so, or in the case of an LLC, examining the Articles of Organization will tell you if this person has the authority.

Summary

In determining ownership, here are some key points to avoid the mistake of buying a home from someone who does not have the exclusive right to sell it to you:

➤ Check public records with the register of deeds to see who has legal title.

➤ Check with the County Assessor to cross check ownership in public tax records, and also see if there are any outstanding taxes or municipal assessments unpaid.

➤ Consult with a Title Company or Abstract Attorney in your State and hire them to perform a title search to verify ownership.

➤ If the property is owned by a legal entity other than an individual, investigate and verify that the person selling to you has the authority to do so.

MISTAKE #3: FAILURE TO GET IT IN WRITING

తుంచి

The definition of a contract is: *a written or spoken agreement, especially one concerning employment, sales, or tenancy that is intended to be enforceable by law.*

The legal definition of an oral contract is: an agreement that is not in writing and is not signed by the parties but is a real existing contract that lacks only the formal requirement of a memorandum to render it enforceable in litigation.

The use of an oral contract could best be described as a tool to conduct business under a short term or simple transaction of goods or services. One could also argue that they are best used for items or services that are low in dollar value.

However, when it comes to an expensive purchase, or a transaction with many details and one that is longer in terms of time to complete, it is best to get the agreement in writing.

As sensible as this may sound, as a Realtor I have encountered many people who have engaged in a land contract arrangement with another party using an oral contract or a contract that covers part of the details, and leaves the remainder to an oral agreement between the parties. This type of situation most often occurs between parties who are familiar with each other as either family or friends.

To better understand the importance of having an agreement in writing, let's examine the three aspects discussed above that would indicate a written agreement should be used: Price, Details and Time.

Price

When it comes to the price of an item, the higher the price the more money is at risk. When one considers the definition of financial risk: the danger or possibility of loss. The more money involved in a transaction, the higher the risk. Therefore, the more one must be certain to minimize risk by getting the agreement in writing so that both parties agree to what is being sold, how it is being sold, what the terms are and who is selling what to whom. A contract will also define when it is to be paid and the remedies for default on such an agreement.

Details

When one begins to discuss details, there is a degree of certain complexity. In order to keep all of the details clear to all parties, especially when the agreement will need to be followed over time, the clearer one can make the agreement the better. That way at a later date, should a detail come into question the written agreement can be consulted and the matter clarified for interested parties.

Time

Time becomes the perhaps the strongest element in any contract. The longer the time involved, the more likely a contract will become a written one as opposed to an oral one. Time brings changes. A seller or buyer in a contract could become deceased, and the ownership interest in the contract could pass to an heir or be subject to probate court. Having a written agreement makes it clear to any subsequent heir or court system what the agreement was, who is involved and what the terms are. This can protect the surviving party in this eventuality, and in so doing demonstrate the enforceability of the contract.

Notarized Signatures

Using a Notary Public is also a recommended step in the signing of any land contract. A Notary Public is: A person authorized by law to take oaths and witness signatures on documents.

In some states, the notary must post a *fidelity bond*. A fidelity bond is a form of insurance that covers the policy holders for losses that they incur as a result of fraudulent or dishonest acts. Additionally, in some states, notaries must keep complete logs of all documents notarized and the type of identification provided by the party signing the instrument.

Using a notary to witness signatures helps both parties in the future should anyone at a later date challenge the authenticity of the signatures in the contract. This can become particularly important as in the example given above when a party in the contract dies. With the contract including notarized signatures, the surviving party has a measure of protection from any challenge to the authenticity of the contract from an heir or court system.

Should a court decide to subpoena a notary public's log book to verify signatures, they can do so. Using a notary public is a free service, and one can find one at most financial institutions such as a bank, credit union or title office.

Emphasis on getting all parts of the transaction in writing

Whenever you are selling a home, a preliminary step to having all parties sign on the Land Contract is to have the agreement with terms of sale in writing. If you use a Realtor, they will help you with the legal purchase agreements and required disclosures in your area.

Purchase Agreements

If you choose to do this yourself, I would suggest you start with a basic purchase agreement. A purchase agreement would outline who the parties are, what the agreed upon sales price is, what the terms of the sale are (The amount being put down, payments, etc.) and details on what each party is going to be responsible for. Define also which party pays closing fees, insurance, escrow, taxes, title verification and inspections.

Other things that may be included in the Purchase Agreement could be home warranties, repairs, and personal property that may be on the premises. The agreement will also address time tables for when all these actions are to be done, and by whom.

The day of final closing should also be defined in the agreement to make sure there is a target all parties are working towards. This day of closing is when the money changes hands, and the actual Land Contract agreement is signed.

Lead Based Paint Disclosure

Federal law requires that all parties in a sale of residential real estate sign a lead based paint disclosure if the home was built before 1978.

The buyer is given a disclosure on this by the seller, and is given an opportunity to pay for additional lead based paint inspections if they desire.

Seller's Disclosures

Individual state laws also mandate that a general 'seller's disclosure' be made available by the seller and reviewed and signed by the buyer as part of the sale. There can be other additional disclosures in each State as well, or ones that pertain to a region, and they can cover many subjects from mine shafts to Air Force flight paths to native American burial sites. Check with your local Board of Realtors or State agency that oversees Real Estate transactions for the area to find out if any are required.

History of Ownership

Title agencies also provide a valuable service in researching a property history of title, and providing title insurance to each party in the transaction.

I always suggest with the purchase of any real estate that one obtain title insurance, as it protects you from ever having someone come along later and claim ownership to your property, or attempting to collect liens on the former owner, etc.

Always get the agreement in writing and signed by all parties before you move forward with the formal Land Contract. As a seller, you should also request verification that the person buying has the funds for down payment; this can be a simple as being presented with a bank statement showing available funds.

It is also customary to require an earnest deposit from the buyer to show they are serious, and in many states any agreement is not a legally binding contract if they do not provide one.

Oral Agreements in the Court System

An oral contract can be admissible in court. The challenge is to prove the oral contract's existence. Some people prefer to do business on a handshake. Believe it or not, the origin of the handshake was to assure both parties that the other was not carrying a gun. With the shaking of hands in an agreement, both parties knew the other was not holding a weapon.

If you are the type of person who prefers informal agreements sealed by a handshake, at the very least, have a few people on hand to witness you "shake on it." A handshake deal is always more binding when there are witnesses to the agreement.

Without witnesses, it becomes more difficult to prove. In other words: *avoid agreeing to a land contract in a dark alley when no one else is looking.* Keep all the names of the people who are there for the "hand shake" and hope they all remember the same terms that you remember about the agreement.

As one can see, this approach has considerable risks. Hoping all parties remember the same agreement alike.

Losing track of your witnesses over time (as some may move away, become incapacitated or die at a later date). Backing up your testimony with witnesses the over a long term oral contract can become tricky if you are required to prove it in court.

If you do engage in an oral contract with a seller, move into the home immediately and keep track of your payments and cancelled checks as the seller deposits them. Having a record of performance on an oral contract can be backed up with records such as this.

Failing to have witness testimony or any actions that verify your handshake deal, you can always present supporting materials such as deposited checks to strengthen your claim. You can also send correspondence to the seller along with the payments, and keep a record of such. Important note: any correspondence between two parties is admissible in court, particularly if it is sent certified mail.

Faxes, emails, letters, memos and receipts will also help establish your handshake deal. If you are particularly uncomfortable drawing up a contract (such as with a family member or friend) a simple "thank you" letter immediately following a handshake is always a good way to establish the terms of your agreement. The recipient will not think of it as possible "evidence," but simply as a polite gesture.

Of course none of this becomes necessary as long as both parties are happy with the arrangement and nobody fails to perform on their word. With a simple transaction, such arrangements can often go smoothly.

However, should the matter ever wind up in court, the burden will be upon you to prove the existence of a land contract. If you have no evidence, and only your own verbal testimony, you could fail to substantiate your case and lose your rights to ownership of the property.

Land Contract Homes ~ 73

Summary

To avoid the mistake of now having a written contract, the following are key points to remember:

➢ The higher the purchase price, the more detailed the agreement and the longer the contract, the more likely the contract should be in writing.

➢ Oral Contracts are admissible in court, but the burden is upon you to prove it exists.

➢ Getting written agreements notarized can prevent a legal challenge to the signatories and ultimate authenticity of the agreement at a later date.

MISTAKE #4: FAILURE TO RECORD THE LAND CONTRACT IN PUBLIC RECORDS

Public records regarding real estate provide a record and proof of ownership of property. The land contract or a one page document that defines the existence of such a contract is called a 'memorandum of a land contract' and should also be recorded. A memorandum states to one and all doing any future title searches on the property that a Land Contract does exist, and it defines the parties, gives the date it was executed, sales price, etc.

As a buyer, you will want to make sure the seller records the Land Contract or memorandum of a land contract at the Register of Deeds, or local Recording entity as required by your County or State. Why should you do this? Because if either the Land Contract or Memorandum is recorded, you can demonstrate more easily an ownership interest in the property and can more easily defend your proof of title to the property should something happen to the seller during your contract period.

Recording a Land Contract or Memorandum will also prevent the seller from subsequently taking out a mortgage on the property without your knowledge. It also may allow one to qualify for certain tax benefits in your State if it is your principle residence. A homestead exemption tax credit is available for a principle residence; however, in order to qualify for one the proof of ownership of the home to the County assessor must be submitted.

The mistake of failing to record a land contract happens quite often. The record is kept in a desk drawer, but neither party records it with the County. This often happens in private agreements where either one or both party does not understand the benefits of doing this.

It can so also happen when a seller is hiding a defect in title ownership or a recorded mortgage already on public record at the assessor.

Here are a few case examples of instances which illustrates the dangers of what can happen when this occurs:

Case #1: The Mortgaged Home

I received a call from a man asking for advice in sorting out problems he was having with a land contract he signed on a home in Detroit. He signed a land contract with a seller on a house he was living in and nothing was recorded at the assessor's office.

He was trying to refinance the house and settle the land contract and discovered that the seller had taken out another mortgage at a later date on the home which was more than he owed on the land contract for the house. Now he was in a conflict with the seller over the final settlement. I advised him to get an attorney.

The omission here was the failure to record the land contract which would have placed in public records either a memorandum or a copy of the land contract which would have shown up during any title research done on the home when the seller was taking out a mortgage. The lack of recording of the land contract made it possible for the mortgage to be processed.

Case #2: The Unfiled Records

A buyer contacted me about a home she had purchased a few years prior on land contract from a friend. She was asking for help in disputing her high property taxes. In my conversation with her she told me that neither she nor the seller had recorded the land contract at the register of deeds. Nor was there a record at the County Assessor's office. Further research revealed that she was not claiming a homestead exemption her property taxes as her principle residence.

I asked her why she was not doing this, as it was clear she owned no other property and was living in the home. She told me that she did not know that she could do this. I gave her some instructions on how to go about getting a memorandum of land contract prepared at a local title company as well as the homestead exemption, and she eventually got the memorandum recorded and was able to claim the homestead exemption and lowered her property taxes by approximately 40% the following year.

Summary

So in review it is easy to see that failing to record a land contract can not only place your ownership interests at risk, it can also result in higher property taxes if it is your principle residence. Here are the key points to remember to avoid this mistake:

> ➤ Record the existence of a land contract either by recording an original copy at the register of deeds and assessor's office, or a memorandum of land contract.

> ➤ Making sure the existence of a land contract shows up in public record can allow you to take advantage of homestead exemption if it is your principal residence, and it can also serve to protect your financial interests in the home.

MISTAKE #5: NOT BEING AWARE OF OR PREPARED FOR A BALLOON PAYMENT

A mistake that I have seen many, many buyers make that have purchased a home on land contract is the failure to be prepared for financing the home when the balloon comes due on the contract. Many land contract agreements are structured so there is a balloon payment at a later date. This can be in two years, three years or even five years. Whatever terms you have negotiated with the seller, there usually exists a future date when a final settlement is due in on large payment.

Essentially balloons exist to shorten the contract to a precise time frame. They allow a seller to offer financing for a period of time, and the buyer has an opportunity to make payments on the home towards interest and principal.

However, where it goes wrong is when a buyer arrives at that point in time where only a few weeks remain and they have not even looked into refinancing.

Land Contracts can be a bridge

Sometimes people utilize a land contract to bridge the gap from a poor credit status and allow time for to improve their credit. This makes a land contract a useful tool to get someone into a home. This use does require that they work on repairing or improving their credit so that when time when balloon comes due there is a smooth transition into refinancing into a loan.

Credit situations can take time to repair, but what is important to understand is that they can be repaired. It does require some education on how to go about doing this, as well as some diligent work to make it come into being. However, it can be done.

There are many books available on credit repair. Some help you step by step through the process. I wrote a book and released it in 2013 entitled 'Going Home... Renting to Home Ownership in 10 Easy Steps'; this covers several chapters on understanding credit and credit repair for the consumer. There are many other books available on this subject that can walk you through the key points you need to understand.

Repairing Credit

The biggest challenge is to roll up one's sleeves and just do the steps needed to fix credit. Sometimes it requires writing letters, or making calls, or setting up a payment plan to clear up old debt.

It may require some economy in some areas of life to free up the funds to pay off and clean up negative items on ones credit history. It could require restructuring how one spends money on a budget each week.

The most important point here is that one cannot neglect at least taking a look at what needs to be done to qualify for a loan prior to the balloon coming due. My recommendation is that soon after the land contact is agreed to, one should seek out a conventional lender and find out where one stands for a future loan.

Experienced lenders can often offer a road map of what steps are needed to become eligible at a future date if disqualified in present time. It would be advisable to have this information before you structure a land contract, so that you can account for the correct amount of time needed to repair or improve on a credit history to make oneself eligible for a future loan.

What happens when you are not prepared for a balloon?

If you come to that point in time where the balloon is due, and you are not prepared to or unable to refinance, there could be two scenarios that could happen:

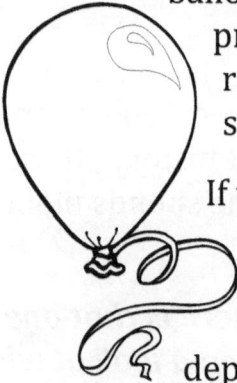

If the seller is unwilling to extend the land contract terms for another period, one could forfeit the investment. It depends on what was agreed to in the contract, and the remedies outline in the contract for this eventuality.

The seller could pursue legal course for *forfeiture of land contract* in the courts. If it is deemed that you are in default by not paying the balloon, you could lose your investment and be ordered to vacate. The property returns to the original seller.

It the seller is willing to extend the contract, new terms would have to be negotiated. This could mean an increase in interest or payments. This may or not work for your budget depending on the situation.

Summary

So in this chapter we examined the importance of not overlooking a future balloon payment in ones financial planning. We also looked at how one can be prepared for this even before an agreement is signed. Here are the key points in this chapter to consider:

➢ Many land contract agreements consist of a future balloon payment in the terms. It is important to know and understand when that is and how much it will be.

➢ One should have a plan worked out before a land contract agreement is signed when a balloon is included on how this sum will be paid when it comes due. This can mean getting with a conventional lender beforehand and working out a plan to improve credit in the future so one can qualify for a new loan.

➢ Be certain you understand the land contract agreement regarding the balloon payment and know what options are available when the balloon comes due should you not be able to perform on this payment requirement. It is best to know in advance, as it will influence your decision on whether the investment in the home is a worthwhile one.

➢ Never commit to a land contract without a sound personal financial plan for settling a future balloon payment.

MISTAKE #6: FAILURE TO VERIFY MARKET VALUES ALIGN WITH THE PURCHASE PRICE

❧

In any real estate transaction one always has an agreed upon purchase price between the seller and the buyer. With land contracts there is no difference. The mistake that is made by many buyers is once again getting caught up in the glow of being able to buy a home and finding out later they paid way too much over market value for the home.

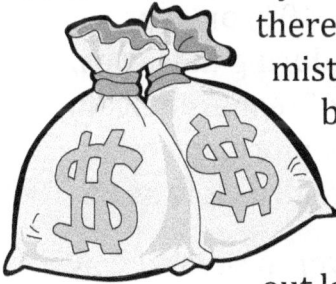

Once an agreement is signed and the land contract is put into effect, it is a legally binding contract. It is much like a conventional mortgage. There is no option available to renegotiate the price short of walking away from it (default).

Paying slightly more for a home as compared to the market value of the area can be justified in markets where the home values are progressively increasing. However, markets can change as the entire country learned in the five years between 2007- 2012 in the U.S., where over a five year period real estate values across the nation in many markets crashed to levels never before expected. Families across the U.S. saw their medium net worth plummet 40% on average during these years with the steep descent of real estate values following the sub-prime mortgage crisis. Some States saw values fall as low as 65-70%.

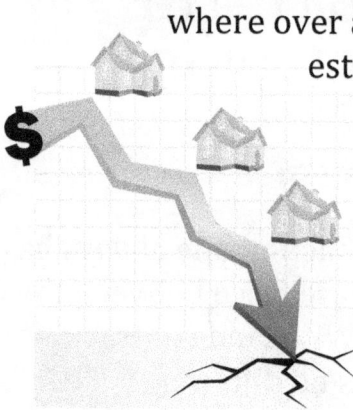

This can impact the buyer in several ways:

- When it comes time to refinance the home and it does not appraise for market values in the area one can fall short of funds one can borrow to pay off or settle a balloon.

- Should one want to sell the home in the future before the land contract is complete, and desire to settle the debt, this could prove to be impossible unless you bring money to the table to settle the difference. New buyers will not be concerned about how much you owe or what you paid for it. They will want to purchase the home at market value.

- It could move the home into a higher property tax bracket due to a higher sale value. This can mean higher tax payments as compared to the other homes in the neighborhood, and not only make it expensive, but unappealing to new buyers should you decide to sell in the future.

Buying a home over market value for an area means one has no equity in the home. Equity is that value assigned between the actual purchase price of the home and the projected resale value as compared to the surrounding market. Homes with a purchase price over market value are said to have a negative equity.

Homeowners seeking to borrow against their homes equity in the future for repairs are unable to do so in a negative equity situation.

This means also that there is no increase in value from the original investment upon future resale, and as stated before one may have to bring additional funds to closing in the event of resale in order to sell the home. This means a loss of one's investment dollars over the years of ownership, no matter the improvements one makes to the home in that time period.

How does one avoid paying more for a home than it is worth?

Here is a list of suggested actions to take as a buyer to verify the purchase price one is paying for a home is within the market value for the area:

- Ask a local Realtor familiar with the market area to provide you with comparables on home sales in that neighborhood of similar size, bedroom count and other features to see what other sale values are that exist.

- Hire an independent appraiser to do a full appraisal on the home. This will cost some money to do, but it is better to spend the money and not buy the home after learning it is overpriced than to blindly purchase the home and lose much more later on because you bought it over market value.

- If one cannot find a Realtor or appraiser, one should go to the public records in that County or Parrish and look for homes that have sold on that street or neighborhood of similar size. Sales values are recorded as a matter of public record. This can be a more tedious approach, but it will serve if the other options are not available to you.

Summary

Paying too much for a home is every buyer's worse fear. This is not only an economic fear, but also a personal one. No one wants to hear from a family member or colleague later on that they made a mistake on such an important step of a purchase. However, it happens. People become desperate for a place to live rather than renting, and the desire to have their own independence can result in them making a poor decision that they later regret.

Here are some key points to retain from this chapter:

- ➢ To protect oneself from paying too much, one should also never be in a rush when buying a home. Follow a comfortable pace through the process. Make sure you investigate and look for yourself.

➢ Do not take everything the seller is telling you as sooth. Remember they are trying to sell their home, and not everyone will disclose all the information you need to know. Involving your own chosen independent professionals is a safe way to do this to get a clear viewpoint.

➢ Do your own research. Investigate for yourself the information presented by the seller. Check public records for market values, or consult a Realtor or Appraiser. Make sure you are comfortable with the market values in the area, and negotiate a sales price that aligns with that value.

➢ Be willing to walk away from a home if the seller is trying to sell it to you for an overpriced value as compared to the market area. Paying too much for a home can become a liability down the road when it comes to refinancing or resale.

MISTAKE #7: NEGLECTING TO USE A TITLE COMPANY OR PAY FOR TITLE INSURANCE

Whenever one is purchasing real estate or any kind, it is prudent to use a Title Company (Note: In some States an *Abstract Attorney* is used). Title Companies are companies that are involved in examining and insuring title claims for real estate purposes.

They investigate the history or '*chain of title ownership*' of a property and look for defects (Anything that could represent a break in the legal chain of title from previous owners).

When they have performed their own investigation to their satisfaction, they issue a form of insurance called '*Title Insurance*'.

Title Insurance is defined as: *A form of indemnity insurance predominantly found in the United States which insures against financial loss from defects in title to real property and from the invalidity or unenforceability of mortgage liens.*

A title insurance policy on a property protects against someone coming along at a later date and claiming ownership. They also protect against liens, suits, etc. related to the history of prior ownership as defined in the title search.

It protects a buyer's interest in the property and covers any cost of legal defense should their title to the property ever be challenged by another party.

Title Insurance is available all over the U.S. It is also available in many countries around the world including: Canada, Australia, the United Kingdom, Mexico, New Zealand, Japan, China, Korea and throughout many countries in Europe.

Prior to the invention of title insurance, homebuyers were solely responsible for ensuring the validity of the land title held by the seller. If the title were later deemed invalid or found to be fraudulent, the buyer lost his investment. The buyer would also bear all legal expense in defending a challenge to land title in the event this happened.

So one can see that it makes a lot of sense to involve a title company and pay for title insurance in the process of purchasing a home. The initial cost far outweighs the liabilities one assumes without this coverage.

However, it is quite common to find buyers of homes on land contract (with a handshake arrangement with a seller or even a written agreement on the sale) to omit the necessity of obtaining title insurance.

When there is a defect in a chain of title, the title is said to be 'clouded'. A clouded title means: *Any irregularity in the chain of title that would give a reasonable person pause before accepting a conveyance of title.*

The discovery of a cloud on title reduces the value and marketability of property because any prospective buyer aware of the cloud will know that they are buying the risk the *grantor* may not be able to convey good title. This can be reason enough for a prospective buyer to back out of a real estate transaction.

To further illustrate the importance of this; here is a list of things that can go wrong in a chain of title which can cause a title to become clouded because of some of the following hidden risks that can be associated with a property in the title search:

- Prior owner had their name spelled wrong on the deed; invalid or wrong owner on deed.

- Legal description of the property has an error in it

- Wrong legal description for the property

- A death certificate not recorded on prior owner who passed away leaving the property to a surviving spouse.

- Forged deeds, mortgages or releases of mortgages and other instruments.

- Liens from unpaid real estate, inheritance, income and gift taxes.

- An IRS lien on the property.

- Legal description not adequate to describe property.

- Undisclosed divorce of spouse who conveys as sole heir of deceased consort.

- An unrecorded land contract.

- Fraud, duress or coercion in securing essential signatures.

- Deeds of persons of unsound mind.

- Invalid, erroneous, suppressed or undisclosed interpretation of wills.

- Defective acknowledgement due to lack of authority of notary. (Acknowledgement taken before commission or after commission has expired.)

- Recorded easement.

This is just a quick list of some of the major things that can cloud a title. As a buyer, title insurance is the most inexpensive type of insurance you will ever have to invest in. You may never need it, however, if you do, it can save you a lot of problems at a later date.

Summary

The essential points about this chapter and how to avoid this mistake are:

> ➢ Use a Title Company when transacting any real estate.

> ➢ Purchase Title Insurance.

MISTAKE #8: DECLINING OR OMITTING TO HAVE THE HOME INSPECTED

In the eagerness of trying to become a homeowner, this is a mistake that many make. A home inspection is the action of hiring a professional who can go through the home and give you a professional analysis of the entire condition of the property and its systems.

A Realtor can help you schedule and arrange inspections. Hiring a professional home inspector will cost money, and the fees will vary depending on what is being inspected, for example, a *General Overall Home Inspection*: Covers most systems like HVAC, Electrical, Plumbing, roof, structural, appliances, etc.

In addition to the general overall home inspector, here is a list of some of the common categories of other inspections that can be done:

Structural Inspection: With some home such as manufactured homes it can be a requirement to get a structural inspection by a licensed engineer to make sure that the home is affixed to its foundation per State safety guidelines.

Termite and Pest Inspection: Checks the home for the presence of wood destroying inspects.

Radon and Methane Gas Inspection: Test for the presence of toxic gases that can be serious health issues.

HVAC system Inspection: Checks the function of the heating and air conditioning systems in the home.

Roof Inspection: Checks the condition and estimates age and prospective lifespan of the existing roof.

Plumbing Inspection: Checks the plumbing systems in the home.

Electrical Inspection: Checks the breaker box and electrical system in the home for code compliance, function and safety.

Swimming Pool and/or Spa Inspection: Checks the condition of swimming pool liners, pumps and other systems. Also can inspection the function of systems related to a spa.

Well Inspection: Tests the water cleanliness of a well as well as compliance with current codes.

Septic Inspections: Checks the sewage levels and condition of system as per current codes.

Chimney Inspection: Safety and function inspection of the chimney and fireplace systems in the home. Some older chimneys do not have liners in the flue which can present a fire hazard. A Chimney inspector will determine if the smoke is discharged properly.

Lead Based Paint Inspection: Specialized testing for the presence of lead based paint in a home. The federal government banned the use of lead based paint in 1978, but homes older than that year may still have exposed lead based paint.

Foundation Inspection: Checks the condition and stability of the foundation of the home.

Soil Toxicity and Stability: Checks the toxicity of the soil on the property. This can be particularly important with agricultural properties or homes adjacent to such properties which can be prone to contamination. This category also checks the soil for stability in certain States where landslides and soil shifting is a common hazard. If you are purchasing a home on the side of a hill, for example, this would be an important inspection so the home does not slide away in a rain storm, etc.

Asbestos Inspection: Checks for the presence of Asbestos in the home.

Mold Inspection: The presence of mold can trigger many health problems. There are many different types of mold that can exist in a home, and not all are toxic.

Formaldehyde Inspection: This is a colorless and flammable gas used in some building products. It has been known to cause cancer in laboratory test rats.

Air Quality Testing: Checking the condition of the air quality in the home for mold and spores.

Property Survey: Verifying the boundaries of the home as per the legal description can expose any encroachments or easements on the land which can impact the resale value as well as the ability to convey title.

Arborist Inspection: Hiring a professional to inspect the trees on the land to for their overall health and condition.

When commissioning a general overall home inspection, it is a good idea to be present during or right after the inspections are done, so that you can benefit from the home inspector walking you through the home and getting oriented to the actual condition of the property.

One can learn a lot about a home one is buying by spending time with the home inspectors that can point out their findings and make you aware of them, as well as educate you on the various functions of the home.

Specialty inspections such as termite and pest inspections should be included on your list as well, and can often be a requirement in certain States (like Georgia, for example).

The discoveries found during inspections can sometimes result in a buyer deciding not to buy a home if the cost of repairs required is too high or the condition is found to be something one cannot live with.

Often you can submit an addendum to the contract which notes adjustments or modifications to the earlier contract, as a result of information uncovered in the inspection process.

Always do a home inspection *before* you commit to a final settlement on a land contract if you are going to do them. Inspecting after the contract has been executed does not guarantee the seller will be agreeable to repairs or adjustments to the home based on findings from the inspection.

You will have more success with negotiating repairs and corrections with a seller if the inspections are done before you sign and agree to the contract with them. Note: *It is always important to stipulate in a purchase agreement that the deal is based on satisfactory inspections.*

Inspections are a vital necessity, so that you can get that third party professional evaluation on the condition of the property you intend to purchase.

Be certain to use a reputable inspector, and if your state requires licensing, then be sure he or she is properly licensed.

It is not rude to ask so see an inspector's license or credentials before you hire them. In fact many expect it, so don't be shy in asking for it.

Home Warrantees

Home Warrantees are a short term protection plan, typically 12-18 months long, that can help protect the buyer against the possibility of emergency repairs to a specific list of items in the home.

This can include the furnace, air conditioning, plumbing, electrical, etc. Whereas homeowners insurance is a protection against larger catastrophic damages from things such as a storm, fire or other natural disasters, a home warrantee addresses items on a much smaller scale with a lower deductible that in most situations is not covered under one's homeowners insurance.

An option when one finds something in a home inspection that is a concern (such as an older, yet functioning furnace) one can purchase a specialized protection plan called a home warrantee. They cover a homeowner against unexpected repairs defined in the warrantee coverage. Such policies cover major systems in the home like HVAC, plumbing, electrical and appliances.

The cost of a home warranty generally runs around $450 to $500 on average for twelve months of coverage. It is also important to not just buy the basic coverage, but to get the additional coverage that includes correcting or updating code violations.

Often times a prior property owner and 'Do It Yourselfer' improperly installed something on the house, and the contractor cannot do the repairs needed without also addressing the code violations. An example of this might be a water heater or furnace that was installed without a required permit. Be sure to check the warrantee policy for this additional coverage option, and sign up for it if it is available.

When filing a claim, Home Warranty companies require that you call when a repair is needed beforehand, and they then authorize you to call a contractor. Sometimes they even have a list of approved contractors in your area to help save you time.

Also, they usually have a 24 hour, 7 day a week call-in center with most of these companies, so you can reach them at odd hours or weekends.

As a Realtor, I always recommend new buyers obtain a Home Warranty for at least the first year they own a home, as it gives that extra measure of protection that may be lacking in homeowners insurance policies.

Summary

In having the home inspected can protect the buyer from hidden defects and problems associated with a new home purchase. It can also be a vital step to orient oneself to the condition of the home and plan for improvements.

Here is a list of key points:

➢ Always inspect the home, and bring in professionals to inspect whenever possible.

➢ Spend time learning from the inspectors you hire. Become familiar with the home and its condition.

> ➢ Use the knowledge from inspections to plan for future upgrades based on their recommendations.

> ➢ Purchase a home warrantee when possible for added protection.

MISTAKE #9: FAILURE TO PURCHASE HOMEOWNERS INSURANCE

ॐक्ष

Looking at natural disaster statistics in the U.S. from 1980 – 2010 there were recorded a total of 640 events including floods, droughts, earthquakes, volcanoes, landslides, wildfires and storm damage. The average people killed per year because of disasters was 12,366 and the total of $17,557,645 in economic damages according to PreventionWeb.net. According to the U.S. Fire Administration website there was a total of 166,600 homes destroyed by fire in the U.S in 2011 as a result of residential cooking, 26,800 caused by electrical malfunctions and another

43,700 caused by home heating related incidents. That is a total of 237,100 homes destroyed by these types of fires in the 2011 alone, almost a 10% increase over previous years.

This does not even include holiday Christmas light incidents, cigarette smoking, non-residential or fires set by arson each year.

Between 2009 -2011 in the U.S. 6,600 fires originated from the garage causing 30 deaths, 400 injuries and over $457 Million dollars in property damage.

Each year, termites and similar pests cause an estimated $30 billion in damage to crops and man-made structures in the U.S. A homeowner who discovers termite damage will spend an average of $3,000 to repair the damage.

To adopt the attitude that it can never happen to you or that disasters only happen to other people is being naïve. Just speak to anyone who lost their home to a natural disaster or fire. In most cases they never saw it coming; nor could they have prevented it.

When one is financing a home through a conventional or government backed mortgage (such as FHA, VA, USDA Rural Development, etc.) terms of final settlement require a home buyer purchase a homeowners insurance policy before closing can be finalized. The policy must take effect immediately at closing of the loan.

Most anyone with an understanding of the value of the replacement cost in real estate would purchase homeowners insurance on a home. Surprisingly enough I have found it is a common practice for private land contract deals between individuals not working with Realtors or other professionals such as an attorney to neglect the necessity to purchase homeowners insurance. In an effort to save out-of-pocket cost, they omit the purchase of a homeowner's insurance policy.

This is a mistake that even homeowners make when they pay off their mortgage as it is no longer a requirement by a lien holder. I have even met landlords who own rental properties free and clear that make this same decision. Leaving a property unprotected in the eventuality of a major disaster such as storm damage or a loss by fire is quite a gamble. It is one thing to do it consciously and decide as an investor to not insure a rental home. It quite another to not insure a principle residence one is making an investment in.

This is a mistake that gets made most often when someone buys a home but has such a limited income that they cannot plan for any additional expense beyond utilities or their land contract payment.

If someone is in this situation and not in a financial position to pay for this coverage, then they really should reconsider their planning on taking the step to purchase this particular home. If their budget it really that tight, what will they do down the road when it is a requirement by a lender in refinancing? As mentioned earlier in another chapter, when a balloon payment comes due, how will they even qualify for a mortgage with such a limited income? How can they afford to keep the home in good repair? The reality is *they will not.*

If a seller is going to sell a home on land contract, an insurance policy should be in place and that they are listed as a principle interested party to be settled with first. To do otherwise is to enter into too much liability.

However, I have seen it both ways with the seller and the buyers being lax on the importance of home owners insurance coverage, and thus it is listed here as a mistake to avoid.

Summary

Homeowners insurance is a practical and sensible way of protecting ones asset. The home you live in that you are purchasing on land contract is best protected with a homeowner's insurance policy. Here are the key points to take from this chapter:

➢ Make is a primary part of your land contract deal whether you are the buyer or the seller to require that homeowner's insurance coverage is in effect.

➢ Homeowners insurance is considerably less costly than having to pay personally for damages as a result of a natural disaster, storm or fire.

MISTAKE #10: FAILURE TO VERIFY OR ENSURE PROPERTY TAXES PAID

৵৽৹

No matter where you decide to buy a home in the U.S. you will have to pay property taxes. Some states are higher than others, but all 50 States have property taxes of some kind.

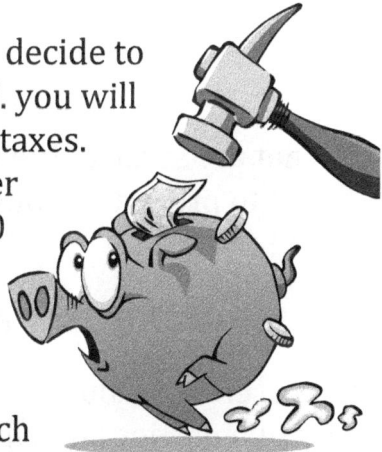

According to a research project by the Tax Foundation on About.com, the top five States where you will pay the least in property taxes is: 1. Louisiana, 2. Hawaii, 3. Alabama, 4. Delaware and 5. West Virginia.

The top five worst States where you will pay the highest are: 1. New Jersey, 2. New

Hampshire, 3. Texas, 4. Wisconsin and 5. Nebraska.

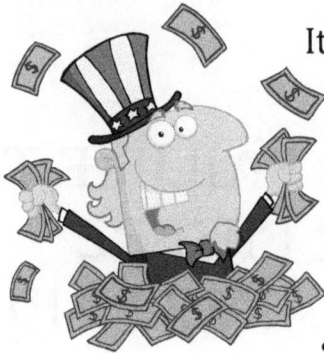

It does not matter where you live in the U.S.; however, a failure to pay property taxes will result in loss of property as most states will sell your property at tax sale to collect delinquent taxes. This brings us to the tenth major mistake I have witnessed in land contract home arrangements: *The neglect or fail to pay property taxes.*

What are some of the ways to ensure these are paid to protect the buyer and the seller in a land contract?

Escrow Accounts

An escrow account is a special account set up by two parties and entrusted to an independent third party who will receive and disburse money from the account for a defined purpose on behalf of the transacting parties. Escrow accounts are set up in real estate agreements to fulfill the function of the payment of property taxes, insurance, homeowner's association fees, etc.

When one purchases a home using a conventional mortgage, quite often the mortgage company sets up an escrow account for the buyer. This escrow arrangement requires the buyer to make a monthly payment in addition to their mortgage payment to cover the cost of the property taxes and homeowners insurance. The totals from these two fees are added together and divided by twelve months to establish this additional payment (Taxes + Insurance/12 Months). Because these the payments for these items are typically either annually or semiannually, the money is placed into a 3rd party account called an 'Escrow' account.

When one is working with seller financing on a land contract, there is no banking institution involved. Keeping track of an escrow payment might be something that neither party may want to be responsible for, but both will have a mutual interest in seeing the taxes and insurance paid.

The solution in this case is to establish an account at an independent escrow service and have the buyer make their monthly taxes and insurance payment directly to them.

The account can be set up to automatically notify the seller that these payments have been made, and provide an account report to both parties annually.

Here is a list of companies that have websites describing how they provide this service. I do not recommend any one company on this list in particular, and one should do their own investigation with the company independently before committing to one.

There may also be others not listed here, so this is by no means a complete list. They are given for sake of example only:

SafeFunds.com

Closeline.com

NationalSoftwareEscrow.com

Escrowserv.com

I suggest a careful study of these websites to gain an understanding of how these service companies function. If you choose to hire one, look for one whose system makes you comfortable. To neglect setting up an Escrow account is to court disaster. Too often one or the other party neglects to pay the property taxes. The home is then sold for back taxes by the State.

Another Important Reason for Using a Title Company

When you hire a title company to help you with closing your land contract they will research the history of taxes.

If there are any unpaid property taxes, they will make it known to both parties so that any back taxes can be settled at closing. When a buyer does not insist upon the use of a title company or attorney in settling the transaction, they run the risk of acquiring a property with unpaid back taxes.

Even if a seller presents proof of payment on all tax bills, there is still the current tax bill to consider. This is another point that buyers sometimes get caught on.

Tax bills are typically annual or semi-annual in their billing cycle. So if you purchase a home in June of 2014, and your seller presents you with a bill showing paid for all taxes in 2013, there are still six months of taxes the seller has not paid in 2014.

Additionally, a person could make a payment equivalent to the 2013 taxes in some cases, but the payment really went to outstanding taxes due in prior years.

Some locations will have multiple property tax billing entities such as the State, County and City or Village. Missing any one of the multiple bills due could result in delinquent taxes and create a future problem with the taxing authority in your State.

So it is important to hire a professional title company to verify the state of property tax bills for you so that you do not get stuck with a tax bill you do not owe.

Summary

Paying property taxes is a part of home ownership. Inescapable if you live in the U.S. and desire to purchase a home. Here are some key points to remember to avoid this mistake in a land contract deal:

➢ Always use professionals to help you establish what taxes are owed, and insist on all back taxes being paid in full up to the date of closing.

➢ Set up and use an escrow company that both parties agree on, and use it to make sure the property taxes, insurance and any other annual fees related to the home are paid from the escrow account directly (i.e. homeowner association dues, annual municipal fees, etc.)

Summary

This section is a compilation of all the key points from all the chapters covering mistakes for your easy access and review. It serves as a quick reference guide for the ten mistakes presented in the preceding chapters.

One can also use this section as a tool for a quick review of any land contract deal one is considering to make sure to not miss any important points.

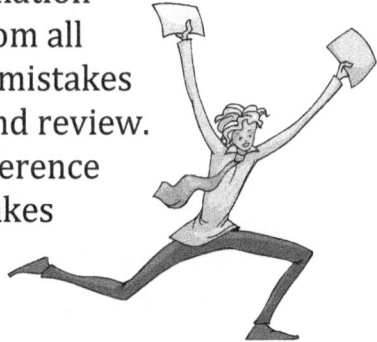

Mistake #1: Lack of General Understanding on Land Contracts

> ➤ Educate yourself on the process and understand how land contracts work. Read books, and most importantly, read

and understand the contract you are being asked to sign.

➢ Consult with professionals who work for you, not for someone else. Ask for their help in reviewing the contract, inspecting the home, or answering basic questions to increase your understanding of the home and the contract you are going to commit to.

➢ Recognize there is a past, present and future with any real estate and its transaction. Take steps to understand each independently.

Mistake #2: Failure to Verify Ownership

➢ Check public records with the register of deeds to see who has legal title.

➢ Check with the County Assessor to cross check ownership in public tax records, and also see if there are any outstanding taxes or municipal assessments unpaid.

➢ Consult with a Title Company or Abstract Attorney in your State and hire them to perform a title search to verify ownership.

➢ If the property is owned by a legal entity other than an individual, investigate and verify that the person selling to you has the authority to do so.

Mistake #3: Failure to get it in Writing

➢ The higher the purchase price, the more detailed the agreement and the longer the contract, the more likely the contract should be in writing.

➢ Oral Contracts are admissible in court, but the burden is upon you to prove it exists.

➢ Getting written agreements notarized can prevent a legal challenge to the signatories and ultimate authenticity of the agreement at a later date.

Mistake #4: Failure to Record the Land Contract in Public Records

➢ Record the existence of a land contract either by recording an original copy at the register of deeds and assessor's office, or a memorandum of land contract.

➢ Making sure the existence of a land contract shows up in public record can allow you to take advantage of homestead exemption if it is your principal residence, and it can also serve to protect your financial interests in the home.

Mistake #5: Not Being Aware of or Prepared For a Balloon Payment

➢ Many land contract agreements consist of a future balloon payment in the terms. It is important to know and understand when that is and how much it will be.

➢ One should have a plan worked out before a land contract agreement is signed when a balloon is included on how this sum will be paid when it comes due. This can mean getting with a conventional lender beforehand and working out a plan to improve credit in the future so one can qualify for a new loan.

➢ Be certain you understand the land contract agreement regarding the balloon payment and know what options are available when the balloon comes due should you not be able to perform on this payment requirement. It is best to know in advance, as it will influence your decision on whether the investment in the home is a worthwhile one.

> Never commit to a land contract without a sound personal financial plan for settling a future balloon payment.

Mistake #6: Failure to Verify Market Values Align with the Purchase Price

> To protect oneself from paying too much, one should also never be in a rush when buying a home. Follow a comfortable pace through the process. Make sure you investigate and look for yourself.

> Do not take everything the seller is telling you as sooth. Remember they are trying to sell their home, and not everyone will disclose all the information you need to know. Involving your own chosen independent professionals is a safe way to do this to get a clear viewpoint.

> Do your own research. Investigate for yourself the information presented by the seller. Check public records for market values, or consult a Realtor or Appraiser. Make sure you are comfortable with the market values in the area, and negotiate a sales price that aligns with that value.

> ➢ Be willing to walk away from a home if the seller is trying to sell it to you for an overpriced value as compared to the market area. Paying too much for a home can become a liability down the road when it comes to refinancing or resale.

Mistake #7: Neglecting to Use a Title Company or Pay for Title Insurance

> ➢ Use a Title Company when transacting any real estate.

> ➢ Purchase Title Insurance.

Mistake #8: Declining or omitting to have the Home Inspected

> ➢ Always inspect the home, and bring in professionals to inspect whenever possible.

> ➢ Spend time learning from the inspectors you hire. Become familiar with the home and its condition.

> ➢ Use the knowledge from inspections to plan for future upgrades based on their recommendations.

> ➢ Purchase a home warrantee when possible for added protection.

Mistake #9: Failure to pay for Homeowners Insurance

➤ Make is a primary part of your land contract deal whether you are the buyer or the seller to require that homeowner's insurance coverage is in effect.

➤ Homeowners insurance is considerably less costly than having to pay personally for damages as a result of a natural disaster, storm or fire.

Mistake #10: Failure to Ensure or Verify Property Taxes Paid

➤ Always use professionals to help you establish what taxes are owed, and insist on all back taxes being paid in full up to the date of closing.

➤ Set up and use an escrow company that both parties agree on, and use it to make sure the property taxes, insurance and any other annual fees related to the home are paid from the escrow account directly (i.e. homeowner association dues, annual municipal fees, etc.)

GLOSSARY OF COMMON OF REAL ESTATE TERMS

ABSORPTION RATE: Describes the ratio of the number of properties in an area that have been sold against the number available. Usually in report form to show the volatility of a market.

ABSTRACT OF TITLE: A compilation of the recorded documents relating to a parcel of land, from which an attorney may give an opinion as to the condition of the title. This system is still in use in some parts of Wisconsin and in some other states; but more often giving way to the use of the system of title insurance. (See also: *TITLE INSURANCE*)

ACCELERATION CLAUSE: A provision in a mortgage that gives the lender the right to demand *immediate payment* of the outstanding loan balance under certain circumstances. This is usually when the borrower defaults on the loan, but is can also be for other terms defined in the mortgage.

ACCREDITED BUYER REPRESENTATIVE (ABR): A professional designation earned by REALTORS® who take advanced training in Buyer Representation offered by the Real Estate Buyer's Agent Council (REBAC). (See also: *REAL ESTATE BUYERS AGENT COUNCIL*)

ACRE: A measurement of an area of land that totals 43,560 square feet.

ACTUAL AGE: The amount of time that has passed since a building or other structure was built. (See also: *EFFECTIVE AGE*)

AD VALOREM TAX: Taxes assessed by a State, County or Municipality based on the value of the land and improvements.

ADDENDUM: A supplement to any document that contains additional information pertinent to the subject. Appraisers use an addendum to further explain items for which there was inadequate space on the standard appraisal form. Something added; a list or other material added to a document, letter, contractual agreement, escrow instructions, etc. (See also: *AMENDMENT*).

ADJUSTABLE-RATE MORTGAGE (ARM): A type of mortgage where the interest rate varies based on a particular index, normally the prime lending rate. A loan in which the rate of interest is tied to a specific financial index, with both the rate of interest and the monthly payments subject to change at established adjustment intervals of time.

ADJUSTED SALES PRICE: An opinion of a property's sales price, after adjustments have been made to account for differences between it and another comparable property.

ADJUSTED INTERVAL: This defines the period of time between the changes in the interest rate and/or monthly payment as part of an 'adjustable rate' loan. These intervals will vary depending on the lending institution and the type of loan for which application is being made.

AFFORDABILITY ANALYSIS: A calculation used to determine an individual's likelihood of being able to meet the obligations of a mortgage for a particular property. This analysis takes into account the down payment, closing costs and on-going mortgage payments, as well as the individual's financial application.

AGENCY: Any relationship in which one party (agent) acts for or represents another (principal) under the authority of the latter. Agency involving real property should be in writing, such as listings, Buyer brokerage agreements, trusts, powers of attorney, etc.

AGENT: A person who has been appointed to act on behalf of another for a particular transaction.

ALTA (American Land Title Association): An organization composed of title insurance companies which have adopted certain insurance policy forms to standardize coverage on a national basis.

AMENDMENT: A change to alter a part of an agreement without changing the principal idea or essence.

AMENITY: Any feature of a property that increases its value or desirability. These might include natural amenities such as location or proximity to mountains, or man-made amenities like swimming pools, parks or other recreation.

AMORTIZATION: The repayment of a loan through regular periodic payments. A payment breakdown for a debt, broken into installment payments; consisting of both principal and interest over a defined period of time. The origin of the word 'Amortize' derives from the Latin meaning of 'To put to death'. So Amortization ultimately means to extinguish or 'put to death' a debt or loan.

AMORTIZATION SCHEDULE: The breakdown of individual payments throughout the life of an amortized loan, showing both principal contribution and debt service (interest) fees. (See *AMORTIZATION*)

AMORTIZATION TERM: The length of time over which an amortized loan is repaid. Mortgages are commonly amortized over 15 or 30 years. (See *AMORTIZATION*)

ANNUAL PERCENTAGE RATE (APR): The rate of annual interest charged on a loan.

APPLICATION: A form used to apply for a mortgage loan that details a potential borrower's income, debt, savings and other information used to determine credit worthiness. It often requires disclosure of financial information and credit history.

APPLICATION FEE: A fee, often non-refundable, charged by the lender to cover costs of processing an application.

APPRAISAL: A "defensible" and carefully documented opinion of value usually by an appraiser. Most commonly derived using recent sales of comparable properties by a licensed, professional appraiser. A written formal estimation of the 'estimated current value' of a home.

APPRAISAL REPORT: The end result of the appraisal process, usually consists of one major, standardized form such as the Uniform Residential Appraisal Report form 1004, as well as all supporting documentation and additional detail information. The purpose of the report is to convey the opinion of value of the subject property and support that opinion with corroborating information.

APPRAISED VALUE: An opinion of the fair market value of a property (as determined by a licensed certified appraiser), following accepted appraisal principals.

APPRAISER: An educated, certified professional with extensive knowledge of real estate markets, values and practices. The appraiser is often the only independent voice in any real estate transaction with no vested interest in the ultimate value or sales price of the property.

APPRECIATION: The natural rise or increase in property value due to market forces.

APR (Annual Percentage Rate): The cost of credit expressed as a yearly rate. It takes into account interest, points and loan origination fee. Since all lenders are required to use the same guidelines in determining APR, this is a good basis for comparing the cost of various loan programs.

ARMS LENGTH TRANSACTION: Any transaction in which the two parties are unconnected and have no overt common interests. Such a transaction most often reflects the true market value of a property.

ASSESSED VALUE: This is a value assigned to real estate, for taxable purposes, by a local jurisdictional tax assessor.

ASSESSMENT: The function of assigning a value to a property for the purpose of levying taxes.

ASSESSMENT RATIO: The comparative relationship of a property's assessed value to market value.

ASSESSMENTS: (1) The estimating of value of property for tax purposes. (2) A levy against property in addition to general taxes. It can be for improvements such as streets, sewers, etc. (3) Charges against unit owners in a condominium by a condo or homeowners association.

ASSESSOR: The jurisdictional official who performs the assessment and assigns the value of a property.

ASSET: Any item of value which a person owns that is considered appreciating in value.

AUTOMATED UNDERWRITING SYSTEM (AUS): This is a computer program that allows a loan officer to enter a potential borrower's information into it from a submitted application and then reviews it. It provides an instant response as to whether the person will qualify for a loan and for which programs. It is considered to be a rapid and impartial system for preliminarily evaluating an applicant's qualification for a loan.

BALLOON MORTGAGE (OR BALLOON NOTE): A mortgage loan in which the monthly payments are not large enough to repay the loan by the end of the term. So at the end of the term, the remaining balance comes due in a single large payment.

BALLOON PAYMENT: This is the final large payment at the end of a mortgage term.

BANKRUPTCY: When a person or business is unable to pay their debts and seeks protection of the state against creditors. Bankruptcies remain on credit records for up to ten years and can prevent a person from being able to get a loan.

BENEFICIARY: A person or entity named to receive the income or property held in a trust. (See TRUST)

BILL OF SALE: A receipt indicating the sale of property. This is a written document that serves as a record, as when one transfers ownership of personal property.

BORROWER: Anyone who borrows money from a lending source.

BREACH (also called Default): Failure to comply with the terms of a contract.

BROKER (REAL ESTATE): An individual who facilitates the purchase of property by bringing together a buyer and a seller. One who engages in any of several sorts of business activities relating to the financing, rental or sale of real property or a business.

BUNGALOW: A one-story, home-style dating from the early twentieth century. This is often characterized by a low-pitched roof.

BUYER'S AGENT (REPRESENTATIVE): A Real Estate Agent that has a contractual relationship to represent a buyer in a real estate transaction.

CAPE COD COLONIAL: A single-story house style made popular in New England. This is often characterized by a steep roof with gables.

CAVEAT EMPTOR: Literally translated from Latin: *"Let the buyer beware."* A common business tenet, where it describes the buyer's responsibility for verifying any and all claims, made by the seller of the property. The buyer assumes all risk in their purchase.

CERTIFICATE OF ELIGIBILITY: A document issued by the Veterans Administration that certifies eligibility for a VA loan.

CERTIFICATE OF TITLE: A document designating the legal owner of a parcel of real estate. This is usually provided by a title or abstract of title company. (See also: *TITLE* and *ABSTRACT OF TITLE*)

CERTIFIED RESIDENTIAL SPECIALIST (CRS): A professional designation program offered to REALTORS® that requires over 70 hours of advanced training, and the sale of 25 homes to achieve. The CRS designation is offered only by the Council of Residential Specialists. (See also: *COUNCIL OF RESIDENTIAL SPECIALISTS*)

CHAIN OF TITLE: The complete history of ownership of a piece of property.

CHARGE-OFFS: Any time a creditor has closed an account and marked the account off as a loss. A designation on a credit report that an account went delinquent, and the closed the account and took it as a loss as opposed to sending it to collections.

CLEAR TITLE: Ownership of property that is not encumbered by any counter-claim or lien.

CLOSING: The process whereby the sale of a property is consummated with the buyer completing all applicable documentation, including signing the mortgage obligation and paying all appropriate costs associated with the sale (See *CLOSING COSTS*). In real estate sales, the procedure in which documents are executed and delivered in return for the payment of the sales price, and the sale (or loan) is completed.

CLOSING COSTS: Describes all appropriate costs generated by the sale of property, which the parties must pay, to complete the transaction. Costs may include appraisal fees, origination fees, title insurance, taxes and any points negotiated in the deal. One-time costs that must be paid before the loan can be "closed" or funded. These costs may include such things as property taxes, insurance, broker's fees, escrow fees, title insurance premium, deed recording fee, title insurance premium, title transfer tax, etc. Escrow instructions will stipulate which portions of the fees are to be paid by Buyer or Seller. An estimate of closing costs will be given to Buyer by the lender within a few days after receiving the loan application. (All or a portion of the closing costs may be financed depending on the loan program.)

CLOSING STATEMENT: The document detailing the final financial arrangement, complete with settlement figures, between a buyer and seller and the costs paid by each.

CO-BORROWER: A second person sharing obligation on the loan and title on the property.

COLLATERAL: An asset which is placed at risk to secure the repayment of a loan.

COLLECTION: The process a lender takes to pursue a borrower who is delinquent on his payments in order to bring the mortgage current again. This includes documentation that may be used in the foreclosure process.

COMMISSION: Compensation earned by a Real Estate Agent for negotiating a purchase or sale of property or otherwise complying with his agency contract.

COMMON AREA ASSESSMENTS: Fees which are charged to the tenets or owners of properties to cover the costs of maintaining areas shared with other tenets or owners. Commonly found in condominium, PUD or office spaces.

COMMON AREAS: Any areas, such as entryways, foyers, pools, recreational facilities or the like, which are shared by the tenets or owners of property nearby. Commonly found in condominium or office spaces.

COMPARABLES: An abbreviated term used by appraisers to describe properties which are similar in size, condition, location and amenities to a subject property whose value is being determined. The Uniform Standards of Professional Appraisal Practice (USPAP) establish clear guidelines for determining a comparable property.

COMPOUND INTEREST: Interest paid on the principal amount, as well as any accumulated interest.

CONCESSIONS: Additional value granted by a buyer or seller to entice another party to complete a deal.

CONDOMINIUM: A development where individual units are owned, but common areas and amenities are shared equally by all owners.

CONSTRUCTION LOAN: A loan made to a builder or home owner that finances the initial construction of a property, but is replaced by a traditional mortgage one the property is completed.

CONTINGENCY: Something that must occur before something else happens. Often used in real estate sales when a buyer must sell a current home before purchasing a new one.

Or, when a buyer makes an offer that requires a complete home inspection before it becomes official.

CONTRACT: A legally binding agreement, oral or written, between two parties.

CONVENTIONAL MORTGAGE: A traditional, real estate financing mechanism that is not backed by any government or other agency (FHA, VA, etc.).

CONVERTIBLE ARM: A mortgage that begins and is adjustable, that allows the borrower to convert the loan to a fixed rate within a specific timeframe.

CONVEYANCE: Transfer of title to land. Includes most instruments by which interest in real estate is created, mortgaged or assigned.

COST OF FUNDS INDEX (COFI): An index of financial institutions costs used to set interest rates for some Adjustable Rate Mortgages.

COUNCIL OF RESIDENTIAL SPECIALISTS (CRS): A national organization based in Chicago, Illinois that provides advanced training for REALTORS®. The Council of Residential Specialists offers a special designation for REALTORS® called 'Certified

Residential Specialist (CRS)' which is earned after over 70 hours of advanced training, and a minimum of 25 homes sold. CRS is affiliated and endorsed by the National Association of REALTORS®. Less than 4% of REALTORS® nationally earn the CRS designation.

COVENANT: A stipulation in any mortgage that, if not met, can be cause for the lender to foreclose.

CREDIT: A loan of money for the purchase of property, real or personal. Credit is either secured by an asset, such as a home, or unsecured.

CREDIT HISTORY: A record of debt and payments on such, past and present. Used by mortgage lenders in determining credit worthiness of individuals.

CREDITOR: A person to whom money is owed.

CREDIT REPORT: A detailed report of an individual's past credit performance, employment and the history of where they have lived. It is prepared by a credit bureau. Used by lenders to determine credit worthiness of individuals.

CREDIT REPOSITORY: Large companies that gather and store financial and credit information about individuals who apply for credit.

CUL-DE-SAC: A dead-end street with only one entrance/exit. Such a street is usually characterized by a circular turn-a-round at the end.

DEBT: An obligation to repay some amount owed. This may or may not be monetary.

DEBT EQUITY RATIO: The ratio of the amount a mortgagor still owes on a property to the amount of equity they have in the home. Equity is calculated at the fair-market value of the home, less any outstanding mortgage debt.

DEED: A document indicating the ownership of a property.

DEED OF TRUST: A document which transfers title in a property to a trustee, whose obligations and powers are stipulated. Often used in mortgage transactions. An instrument used in many states in place of a mortgage. Property is transferred to a trustee by the borrower (trustor), in favor of the lender (beneficiary), and re-conveyed upon payment in full.

DEED OF RECONVEYANCE: A document which transfers ownership of a property from a Trustee back to a borrower who has fulfilled the obligations of a mortgage.

DEFAULT: The condition in which a borrower has failed to meet the obligations of a loan or mortgage.

DELINQUENCY: The state in which a borrower has failed to meet payment obligations on time.

DEPOSIT: Cash given along with an offer to purchase property, also called earnest money. (See *EARNEST DEPOSIT)*

DEPRECIATION: The natural decline in property value due to market forces or depletion of resources.

DETACHED SINGLE-FAMILY HOME: A single building improvement intended to serve as a home for one family.

DISCOUNT POINTS: Points paid in addition to the loan origination fee to get a lower interest rate. One point is equal to one percent of the loan amount.

DUE-ON-SALE CLAUSE: A clause in a mortgage giving the lender the right to demand payment of the full balance when the borrower sells the property.

DUPLEX: A single-building improvement which is divided and provides two units which serve as homes to two families.

DWELLING: A house or other building which serves as a home.

DOWN PAYMENT: An amount paid in cash for a property, with the intent to mortgage the remaining amount due.

EARNEST MONEY DEPOSIT: A cash deposit made to a home seller to secure an offer to buy the property. This amount is often forfeited if the buyer decides to withdraw his offer. It shows good faith that the transaction proposal will be honored.

EASEMENT: The right of a non-owner of property to exert control over a portion or all of a property. For example, power companies often own an easement over residential properties for access to their power lines, or two properties adjacent to each other might share a common driveway.

ECONOMIC DEPRECIATION: The decline in property value caused by external forces, such as neighborhood blight or adverse development.

EFFECTIVE AGE: The subjective, estimated age of a property based on its condition, rather than the actual time since it was built. Excessive wear and tear can cause a property's effective age to be greater than its actual age.

EMINENT DOMAIN: The legal process whereby a government can take ownership of a piece of property in order to convert it to public use. Often, the property owner is paid fair-market value for the property.

ENCROACHMENT: A building or other improvement on one property which invades another property or restricts its usage.

ENCUMBRANCE: A claim against a property. Examples are mortgages, liens and easements. A claim, lien, charge, or liability attached to and binding real property. Any 'right to' or 'interest in', land which may exist in one other than the owner, but which will not prevent the transfer of fee title.

EQUAL CREDIT OPPORTUNITY ACT (ECOA): U.S. federal law requiring that lenders afford people equal chance of getting credit without discrimination based on race, religion, age, sex etc.

EQUITY: The difference between the fair market value of a property and that amount an owner owes on any mortgages or loans secured by the property.

EQUITY BUILD-UP: The natural increase in the amount of equity an owner has in a property, accumulated through market appreciation and debt repayment.

ESCROW: An amount retained by a third party in a trust to meet a future obligation. Often used in the payment of annual taxes or insurance for real property.

ESCROW ACCOUNT: An account setup by a mortgage servicing company to hold funds with which to pay expenses such as: homeowners insurance and property taxes.

ESCROW AGENT: A neutral third party, appointed to act as custodian for documents and funds.

ESCROW ANALYSIS: An analysis performed by the lender (usually once each year), to see that the amount of money going into the escrow account each month is correct for the forecasted expenses.

ESCROW DISBURSEMENTS: The payout of funds from an escrow account to pay property expenses: such as taxes and insurance.

ESTATE: The total of all property and assets owned by an individual.

ESTOPPELS: The prevention of one from asserting a legal right because of prior actions inconsistent with its assertion.

EXAMINATION OF TITLE: The report on the title of a property from the public records or an abstract of the title. (See also: *TITLE COMPANY* and *ABSTRACT OF TITLE)*

EXCLUSIVE LISTING: An agreement between the owner of a property and a real estate agent giving the agent exclusive right to sell the property.

EXECUTOR: The person named in a will to administer the estate.

FAÇADE: The front exposure of any building. This is often used to describe an artificial or false front which is not consistent with the construction of the rest of the building.

FAIR CREDIT REPORTING ACT: Federal laws, regulating the way credit agencies disclose consumer credit reports. It defines the remedies available to consumers for disputing and correcting mistakes on their credit history.

FAIR HOUSING: This refers to Federal and State laws that embrace the ideal of equal housing opportunities for everyone. *Fair Housing laws* prohibits anyone in the profession of real estate, or mortgage lending from refusing to negotiate for or engage in a real estate transaction with a person because of race, color, religion, national origin, age, sex, familial status, marital status, or mental and physical handicap. In some states, this list is further expanded to include height, weight, sexual orientation and HIV Positive. Discrimination in the terms of a rental, lease, or purchase is against the law. It also includes in the furnishing of facilities in connection with such as a transaction, such as appraising a home, property inspections, land surveys, etc. This also extends to publishing or advertising, directly or indirectly, or intent to make a limitation, specification or discrimination based on any of the categories listed above. The origin of these civil rights goes back to the Civil Rights Act of 1866. It was later expanded with the Civil Rights Act of 1968, and the later the 'Persons with Disabilities Civil Rights Act' of 1976. Many states have followed with their own civil rights acts pertaining to each state constitution.

FAIR MARKET VALUE: The price at which two unrelated parties, under no duress, are willing to transact business. Amount of money for which property will sell following negotiations between the owner of such property who will sell but is not required to sell and a proposed Buyer for such property who is not obligated to buy such property.

FANNIE MAE: A private, shareholder-owned company that works to make sure mortgage money is available for people to purchase homes. Created by Congress in 1938, Fannie Mae is the nation's largest source of financing for home mortgages.

FEDERAL DEPOSIT INSURANCE CORPORATION (FDIC): The U.S. Government agency created in 1933 which maintains the stability of and public confidence in the nation's financial system by insuring deposits and promoting safe and sound banking practices.

FEDERAL HOUSING ADMINISTRATION (FHA): A sub-agency of the U.S. Department of Housing and Urban Development created in the 1930's to facilitate the purchase of homes by low-income, first-time home buyers. It currently provides federally-subsidized mortgage insurance for private lenders.

FHA MORTGAGE: A mortgage that is insured by the Federal Housing Administration (FHA).

FICO: 'FICO' is an acronym for 'Fair, Isaac and Company'. Fair, Isaac & Co. developed the credit scoring system that is used today by the three major credit bureaus: Experian, TransUnion and Equifax.

FIRST MORTGAGE: The description of the primary loan or mortgage secured by a piece of property.

FIXED-RATE MORTGAGE (FRM): A mortgage which has a fixed rate of interest over the life of the loan.

FIXTURE: Any piece of personal property which becomes permanently affixed to a piece of real property. It generally refers to property that it attached to the home, such as light fixtures, toilets, counter tops, etc.

FLOOD INSURANCE: This describes supplemental insurance which covers a home owner for any loss due to water damage from a flood. This is often required by lenders for homes located in federally designated flood zones.

FLOODPLAIN: The extent of the land adjoining water which, because of its topography, would flood if the water overflowed its banks.

FLOOR PLAN: The representation of a building which shows the basic outline of the structure, as well as detailed information about the positioning of rooms, hallways, doors, stairs and other features. Often includes detailed information about other fixtures and amenities.

FORECLOSURE: The process whereby a lender can claim the property used by a borrower to secure a mortgage and sell the property to meet the obligations of the loan.

FORFEITURE: The loss of property or money due to the failure to meet the obligations of a mortgage or loan secured by that property.

FUNCTIONAL OBSOLESCENCE: A decrease in the value of property due to a feature or lack thereof which renders the property undesirable. Functional obsolescence can also occur when the surrounding area changes, rendering the property unusable for it's originally intended purpose.

GENERAL LIEN: A broad-based claim against several properties owned by a defaulting party.

GOVERNMENT MORTGAGE: Any mortgage insured by a government agency, such as the FHA or VA.

GRANTEE: Any person who is given ownership of a piece of property by another party or entity.

GRANTOR: Any person who gives away ownership of a piece of property.

HAZARD INSURANCE: This is insurance covering damage to a property caused by hazards such as fire, wind and accident.

HAZARDOUS MATERIALS: Substances that may be hazardous to health (i.e., asbestos, radon gas, lead based paint).

HOME EQUITY LINE OF CREDIT (HELOC): A type of mortgage loan that allows the borrower to draw cash against the equity in his home.

HOME INSPECTION: A complete examination of a building to determine its structural integrity and uncover any defects in materials or workmanship which may adversely affect the property or decrease its value.

HOME INSPECTOR: A person who performs professional home inspections. This is usually a professional with an extensive knowledge of houses and their construction methods. Their knowledge will also include common house problems, how to identify those problems and how to correct them.

HOMEOWNER'S ASSOCIATION: An organization of home owners in a particular neighborhood or development formed to facilitate the maintenance of common areas and to enforce any building restrictions or covenants.

HOMEOWNER'S INSURANCE: A policy which covers a home owner for any loss of property due to accident, intrusion or hazard.

HOMEOWNER'S WARRANTY: An insurance policy covering the repair of systems and appliances within the home for the coverage period.

HUD-1 SETTLEMENT STATEMENT: A standardized, itemized list, published by the U.S. Department of Housing and Urban Development (HUD), of all anticipated CLOSING COSTS connected with a particular property purchase.

IMPROVEMENTS: Any item added to vacant land with the intent of increasing its value or usability.

INCOME PROPERTY: A piece of property whose highest and best use is the generation of income through rents or other sources.

INDEMNIFY: To make payment for a loss.

INDEPENDENT APPRAISAL: An estimation of value created by a professional, certified appraiser with no vested interest in the value of the property.

INDEX: Used by lenders to calculate the interest adjustments on adjustable rate loans. Some indexes are more volatile than others; this can affect adjustments in the interest rate and, subsequently, the monthly payment. Because these indexes reflect the general movement of interest rates, they tend to keep the rate on an adjustable rate loan in line with market conditions.

INITIAL RATE: An interest rate charged for the first six or twelve months of an adjustable rate loan. Normally this rate will be lower than prevailing fixed market rates.

INSPECTION: The examination of a piece of property, its buildings or other amenities.

INSTALLMENT LOAN: A line of credit for a fixed sum, with pre-set monthly payments including principle and interest. Example: loans for vehicles or equipment.

INSURABLE TITLE: The title to property which has been sufficiently reviewed by a title insurance company, such that they are willing to insure it as free and clear.

INTEREST RATE: A percentage of a loan or mortgage value that is paid to the lender as compensation for loaning funds.

INTEREST RATE CAP: A safeguard built into an adjustable rate loan to protect the consumer against dramatic increases in the rate of interest and, consequently, in the monthly payment. For example, an adjustable rate loan may have a two percentage point limit per year on the amount of increase or decrease, as well as a five percentage point limit (increase or decrease) over the life of the loan.

INTERIM FINANCING: Temporary financing usually for construction or bridge loans to facilitate the purchase of a new home before the sale of the previous home has been closed.

INVESTMENT PROPERTY: Any piece of property that is expected to generate a financial return. This may come as the result of periodic rents or through appreciation of the property value over time.

JOINT TENANCY: A situation where two or more parties own a piece of property together. Each of the owners has an equal share, and may not dispose of or alter that share without the consent of the other owners.

JUDGMENT: An official court decision. If the judgment requires payment from one party to another, the court may put a lien against the payees property as collateral.

JUDICIAL FORECLOSURE: A type of foreclosure conducted as a civil suit in a court of law.

JUNIOR MORTGAGE: A mortgage, such as a second mortgage, which is subordinate as security to another mortgage.

LAND CONTRACT: Describes an installment contract for the sale of land. The Seller (vendor) has legal title until paid in full. The Buyer (vendee) has equitable title during the contract term. See the Author's other book: *Understanding Land Contract Homes: In Pursuit of the American Dream.*

LATE CHARGE: An extra charge, or penalty added to a regular mortgage payment when the payment is made late by an amount of time specified in the original loan document.

LATENT DEFECTS: Any defect in a piece of property which is not readily apparent, but which has an impact of the value. Structural damage or termite infestation would be examples of latent defects.

LEASE: A contract between a property owner and a tenant specifying the payment amount, terms and conditions, as well as the length of time the contract will be in force.

LEASE OPTION: A lease agreement that gives the tenant an option to buy the property. Usually, a portion of the regular monthly rent payment will be applied towards the down payment.

LEGAL DESCRIPTION: The description of a piece of property, identifying its specific location in terms established by the municipality or other jurisdiction in which the property resides. This is often related in specific distances from a known landmark or intersection.

LEGAL NOTICE: The notice required by law in a particular case. It may be actual notice, constructive notice, etc.

LENDER: In real estate, the person or entity who loans funds to a buyer. In return, the lender will receive periodic payments, including principal and interest amounts. It can also be any person or organization that loans money to a borrower.

LENGTH OF CREDIT HISTORY: The length of time a borrower has had established credit accounts that are reported on his/her credit report.

LIABILITIES: A person's outstanding debt obligations.

LIABILITY INSURANCE: Insurance that covers against potential lawsuit brought against a property owner for alleged negligence resulting in damage to another party.

LIEN: Any claim against a piece of property resulting from a debt or other obligation.

LISTING AGENT: The term for a Real Estate agent that has an 'exclusive right to sell' contract with a seller to sell their home. The home is considered to be 'listed' for sale through a Real Estate agent.

LOAN: Money borrowed, to be repaid with interest, according to the specific terms and conditions of the loan.

LOAN OFFICER: A person that "sells" loans, representing the lender to the borrower, and the borrower to the lender.

LOAN ORIGINATION: How a lender refers to the process of writing new loans.

LOAN SERVICING: The processing of payments, mailing of monthly statements, management and disbursement of escrow funds, etc. Typically carried out by the loan company you make payments to.

LOAN-TO-VALUE RATIO (LTV): The comparison of the amount owed on a mortgaged property to its fair market value.

LOCK-IN: An agreement between a lender and a borrower, guaranteeing an interest rate for a loan if the loan is closed within a certain amount of time.

LOCK-IN PERIOD: The amount of time the lender has guaranteed an interest rate to a borrower.

MANUFACTURED HOUSING: Once known as "mobile homes," manufactured housing is any building which has been constructed off site, then moved onto a piece of real property.

MATURITY: The date on which the principal balance of a financial instrument becomes due and payable.

MERGED CREDIT REPORT: A credit report derived from data obtained from multiple credit agencies. This usually is contains information from all three credit bureaus in a single report.

METES AND BOUNDS: A traditional way of describing property, generally expressed in terms of distance from a known landmark or intersection, and then following the boundaries of the property back to its origin.

MILL RATE: A percentage applied to the assessed valuation to determine taxes.

MORTGAGE: A financial arrangement wherein an individual borrows money to purchase real property and secures the loan with the property as collateral.

MORTGAGE BANKER: This describes a financial institution that provides primary and secondary mortgages to home buyers.

MORTGAGE BROKER: This is a person or organization that serves as a middleman to facilitate the mortgage process. Brokers often represent multiple mortgage bankers and offer the most appropriate deal to each buyer.

MORTGAGEE: The entity that lends money in a real estate transaction.

MORTGAGE INSURANCE: This describes a policy that fulfills the obligations of a mortgage when the policy holder defaults, or is no longer able to make payments. The policy protects the mortgage lender.

MORTGAGE INSURANCE PREMIUM (MIP): A fee that is often included in mortgage payments that pays for mortgage insurance coverage.

MORTGAGE LIFE INSURANCE: A policy that fulfills the obligations of a mortgage when the policy holder dies.

MORTGAGE NOTE: A promissory note secured by a mortgage and executed by mortgagor at the same time as the mortgage for the amount stated in the mortgage, with the legal description of land described in the mortgage also stated in such note.

MORTGAGOR: The entity that borrows money in a real estate transaction.

NEIGHBORHOOD: 1) A community, district or area especially with regards to some point of reference. 2) The people living near and around a community.

NOTE: A legal document that obligates a borrower to repay a mortgage loan at a stated interest rate during a specified period of time.

NOTICE OF DEFAULT: Formal written notice from a lender to a borrower that default has occurred.

OCCUPANCY: A physical presence within and control of a property.

OLD TERMITE ACTIVITY: Where no termites are currently active, but indications of past activity can be seen.

OPEN ACCOUNTS: Credit accounts that are open and still in use by a borrower. Accounts considered active and in use by the creditor.

OWNER OCCUPIED: The state of property wherein the owner occupies at least some portion of the property.

PAYMENT HISTORY: The running record of a borrowers' performance on paying back borrowed funds.

PERSONAL PROPERTY: Owned items which are not permanently affixed to the land.

PERSONAL OR 'PRINCIPLE' RESIDENCE: The primary domicile where a person or family lives.

PITI: Refers to 'principal', 'interest', 'taxes', and 'insurance'. This describes the complete monthly home loan payment, inclusive of taxes and insurance.

PLAT: A plan or chart of a piece of land which lays out existing or planned streets, lots or other improvements.

POINT: A percentage of a mortgage amount (one point = 1 percent).

POINTS AND FEES: A point is a charge equal to one percent of the principal amount of the loan (e.g., 2 points charged on a $100,000 loan would> equal $2,000). Points are generally payable at closing and may be paid by the Buyer or Seller, or split between them. In addition, a flat dollar amount fee may also be charged. Under some lending programs, a buyer may be allowed to include these points and fees as part of the total amount financed.

PRE-APPROVAL: The process of applying for a mortgage loan and becoming approved for a certain amount at a certain interest rate before a property has been chosen. Pre-approval allows the borrower greater freedom in negotiations with sellers. It does not mean they have been fully approved for a loan, but just states they have met the preliminary lending requirements and been told so by a lender.

PREPAYMENT: Payment made that reduces the principal balance of a loan before the due date and before the loan has become fully amortized.

PREPAYMENT CLAUSE: Clause in mortgage, mortgage note or land contract providing that debtor may pay more than agreed installment payment at any time.

PREPAYMENT PENALTY: A fee that may be charged to a borrower who pays off a loan before it is due.

PRE-QUALIFICATION: Less formal that pre-approval, pre-qualification usually means a written statement from a loan officer indicating his or her opinion that the borrower will be able to become approved for a mortgage loan.

PRIME RATE: The interest rate that a bank and other lending institutions charge other banks or preferred customers.

PRINCIPAL: The amount owed on a mortgage which does not include interest or other fees.

PRINCIPAL BALANCE: The outstanding balance of principal on a mortgage. This does not include the amount of total interest due.

PRIVATE MORTGAGE INSURANCE (PMI): A form of mortgage insurance provided by private, non-government entities. This is normally required when the loan to value ratio is less that 20%. The premium is paid by the borrower and is included in the mortgage payment. (See also: *LOAN TO VALUE RATIO*)

PROCESSING (TURNAROUND) TIME: The amount of time required from the day loan application documents are submitted in full to the day the loan closes and loan funds are disbursed. This is the total processing time for a home loan.

PROPERTY: Any item which is owned or possessed.

PRO-RATE: To allocate between Seller and Buyer their proportionate share of an obligation paid or due.

PUBLIC RECORDS: Any record recorded by a County or State. These can include judicial records, bankruptcies, foreclosures, deeds, etc.

PURCHASE AGREEMENT: A written contract signed by the buyer and seller stating the terms and conditions under which a property will be sold.

QUIT-CLAIM DEED: A legal document which transfers any ownership an individual has in a piece of property. Often used when the amount of ownership is not known or is unclear.

RANCH HOUSE: An architectural style typified by a single-story, low-roof construction popular in the western U.S.

RATE LOCK (OR GUARANTEE): A guarantee from a lender of a specific interest rate for a period of time.

REAL ESTATE: A piece of land and any improvements or fixtures located on that land.

REAL ESTATE AGENT: A licensed professional who facilitates the buying and selling of real estate.

REAL ESTATE BUYERS AGENT COUNCIL (REBAC): A national organization that offers a special designation for REALTORS® on Buyer Representation in real estate transactions. To earn the designation requires approximately 40 hours of training, in addition to participating in at least 5 transactions as a Buyers Representative. The designation offered by REBAC is entitled 'Accredited Buyer Representative (ABR)' (See also: *ACCREDITED BUYER REPRESENTATIVE*)

REAL ESTATE SETTLEMENT PROCEDURES ACT (RESPA): A federal law requiring lenders to give full disclosure of closing costs to borrowers.

REAL PROPERTY: Land, improvements and appurtenances, and the interest and benefits thereof.

REALTOR®: A designation given to a real estate licensee who is a member of a board associated with the National Association of REALTORS®.

RECORDER: A local government employee whose role it is to keep records of all real estate transactions within the jurisdiction.

RECORDING: The filing of a real estate transaction with the appropriate government agent. A real estate transaction is considered final when it is recorded. (See *RECORDER*)

REMAINING BALANCE: The amount of principal, interest and other costs that has not yet been repaid.

RESIDENTIAL PROPERTY: A piece of property whose highest and best use is the maintenance of a residence.

REVOLVING CREDIT: A type of credit that allows the borrower to make charges against a predetermined line of credit. The customer then pays monthly installments on the amount borrowed, plus interest. Example: Credit Cards are considered revolving lines of credit.

RURAL: An area outside of an established urban area or metropolitan district.

SALE PRICE: The actual price a property sells for, exclusive of any special financing concessions.

SECOND MORTGAGE: A loan secured by the equity in a home, when a primary mortgage already exists.

SECURED LOAN: This is a loan that is backed by collateral. In the case of a mortgage loan, the collateral is the house.

SEPTIC INSPECTION: An inspection of the septic system of a given property. Sometimes this is a required inspection for closing in a contract.

SERVICING: Mortgage bankers typically retain the right to collect monthly payments and take care of any customer problems. They send a payment to the investor each month. For this service, the mortgage banker receives a small fee (1/4% to 1/2% of the mortgage amount).

SINGLE-FAMILY PROPERTY: A property designed and built to support the habitation of one family.

SUBDIVISION: A residential development that is created from a piece of land which has been subdivided into individual lots.

SUBJECT PROPERTY: This is a term which indicates a property which is being appraised.

SURVEY: A specific map of a piece of property which includes the legal boundaries and any improvements or features of the land. Surveys also depict any rights-of-way, encroachments or easements.

SWEAT EQUITY: The method whereby a home owner develops equity in a property, either during the purchase or throughout its life, by personally constructing improvements rather than paying to have them built.

TERM: The number of years before a loan is scheduled to be paid off. 15-year and 30-year terms are most common.

TERMITE LETTER: An official letter from a certified pest inspection company. The letter states that a property has been inspected and found to have been treated, or free and clear of termite infestation. Some States require such a letter for all real estate closings before transfer of title can occur.

TITLE: A specific document which serves as proof of ownership.

TITLE COMPANY: An organization which researches and certifies ownership of real estate before it is bought or sold. Title companies also act at the facilitator ensures all parties are paid during the real estate transaction.

TITLE INSURANCE: A policy which insures a property owner should a prior claim arise against the property after the purchase has been completed. This also covers a lender should a question of ownership arise.

TITLE SEARCH: The process whereby the Title Company researches a properties title history and ensures that no outstanding claims exist.

TRANSFER OF OWNERSHIP: Any means by which the ownership of a property changes hands.

TRANSFER OF TAX: Taxes payable when title passes from one owner to another.

TRANSFER TAX OR TRANSFER FEE: A tax on the transfer of real property. Generally based on value of property being transferred (i.e., purchase price). Check statutes for each state. This is also called 'Documentary Transfer Tax' in some States.

TRUST: A legal entity created by a 'Trustor' to place an estate or property in the care of another called a 'Trustee'. A Trustee oversees the responsibility to manage a Trust for the benefit of the 'Beneficiary', who is the party that will receive the estate or property if the Trust is dissolved.

TRUSTEE: A fiduciary who holds or controls property for the benefit of another.

TRUSTOR: A person who creates a Trust. (See *TRUST*)

TRUTH IN LENDING: A federal law requiring full disclosure by lenders to borrowers of all terms, conditions and costs of a mortgage.

TUDOR: A style of architecture typified by exposed stone, wood and brick construction. This is similar in style to English manor homes.

UNDERLYING FINANCING: A mortgage, deed of trust, land contract etc. Prior to (underlying) a land contract, mortgage, etc. on the same property.

UNDERWRITER: This is a person who works for a lending or some other financial company, and oversees the process of a loan, and makes sure a borrower who is applying complies and conforms to the guidelines as defined by the institution they work for. They often have final approval or disapproval authority on any application.

UNENCUMBERED PROPERTY: Any property which has no outstanding claims or liens against it.

USURY: Charging more than the legal rate of interest for the use of money.

VA GUARANTEE MORTGAGE: A mortgage that is guaranteed by the Department of Veterans Affairs (VA).

VETERANS AFFAIRS, DEPARTMENT OF (VA): The successor to the Veteran's Administration, this government agency is responsible for ensuring the rights and welfare of our nation's veterans and their dependents. Among other duties, the VA insures home loans made to veterans.

VESTING: Name(s) in which title property is held.

WALK-THROUGH INSPECTION: A process whereby an appraiser examines a property in preparation for estimating its value. Also, the process of inspecting a property for any damage prior to that property being bought or sold. Sometimes called a 'final walk-through' when buyers do a final review or tour of a home prior to closing.

WARRANTY: An affidavit given to stipulate the condition of a property. The person giving the warranty assumes liability if the condition turns out to be untrue.

WARRANTY DEED: This is a deed used in many states to convey fee title to real property. Until the widespread use of title insurance, the warranties by the grantor were very important to the grantee. When title insurance is purchased, the warranties become less important as a practical means of recovery by the grantee for defective title.

WEAR AND TEAR: A term used to indicate the normal damage inflicted on a property through every-day use.

WELL INSPECTION: An official inspection of the water quality and functionality of a well system. This is sometimes a required inspection for a closing in some States.

ZONE: A specific area within a municipality or other jurisdiction which conforms to certain guidelines regarding the use of property in the zone. Typical zones include single-family, multi-family, industrial, commercial and mixed-use.

USEFUL LINKS & REFERENCES

᭜

Foreclosure Laws by State:

www.realtytrac.com/foreclosure-laws/foreclosure-laws-comparison

Online Legal Websites for Real Estate forms:

Legal Zoom

www.legalzoom.com

Rocket Lawyer

www.rocketlawyer.com

Law Depot

www.lawdepot.com

Nolo

www.nolo.com

U.S. Legal Forms

www.USLegalForms.com

Legalwiz

www.legalwiz.zom

Resources for Escrow Services

SafeFunds.com

Closeline.com

NationalSoftwareEscrow.com

Escrowserv.com

Paysafeescrow.com

Greenescrow.biz

Resources for Selling a Land Contract:

Amerifunds

www.amerifunds.us

Mortgage Note Buyer US

www.mortgagenotebuyer.us

Cash Flow Connection Pro LLC

www.cashflowconnectionpro.net

Credit Report:

Annual Credit Report

www.annualcreditreport.com

My Fico

www.MyFICO.com

Credit Repair Information:

Federal Trade Commission Consumer Information on Credit Repair: www.consumer.ftc.gov

Reports on Credit Repair: www.BankRate.com

1031 Tax Deferred Exchanges:

1031 Tax Deferred Exchange Made Simple

www.1031exchangemadesimple.com

1031.org FAQ Page

www.1031.0rg/about1031/faq.htm

1031 Investing inside a Roth IRA

www.1031fec.com/RithIRA.htm

1031 Exchange Advantage FAQ Page

www.1031exchangeadvantage.com

1031 Exchange Institute

www.1031exchangeinstitute.org

About the Author

Michael Delaware is a Phoenix, Arizona native who now resides in Battle Creek, Michigan with his wife Margarita. He also lived in Georgia for 15 years in the 1980's and 1990's where he owned and operated a stained and beveled glass studio in the Metro-Atlanta area. During those years he was an active volunteer in the community, coordinating annual Arts and Crafts Festivals in the downtown district of Roswell, Georgia. He also participated in Arts & Crafts Shows for over

25 years as a vendor in numerous States. He has been a Michigan resident since 1999.

His other published works include numerous non-fiction books on real estate, sales management, marketing and other self-help topics. He has also published fiction and non-fiction stories for children

As an illustrator and photographer, he has included his works in his own books and blogs. He enjoys hiking and mountain biking in the great outdoors and taking long walks in the woods with his dog.

Currently he is an active Realtor in Michigan and frequent community volunteer. He is a member of the National Association of Realtors, The Council of Residential Specialists, and the Michigan Association of Realtors. He is also an active member of the Battle Creek Area Association of Realtors where he was awarded 'Realtor of the Year' in 2010, and served as Board President in 2011. He founded his own independent publishing company in 2012.

To follow Michael:

www.MichaelDelaware.com

Facebook.com/MichaelDelawareAuthor

Amazon.com/Author/MichaelDelaware

Linkedin.com/in/MichaelDelaware

@MichaelDelaware

Other titles by the author available as eBooks:

The Art of Sales Management: Lessons Learned on the Fly *(also available in paperback)*

The Art of Sales Management: Revelations of a Goal Maker *(also available in paperback)*

The Art of Sales Management: 75 Training Drills to Build Confidence, Excellence & Teamwork *(also available in paperback)*

Small Business Marketing: An Insider's Collection of Secrets *(also available in paperback)*

Arts & Craft Shows: The Top 10 Mistakes Artist Vendors Make... And How to Avoid Them! *(also available in paperback)*

Arts & Craft Shows: 12 Secrets Every Artist Vendor Should Know *(also available in paperback)*

Inspiration: The Journey of a Lifetime

For Real Estate:

Understanding Land Contract Homes: In Pursuit of the American Dream *(also available in paperback)*

Land Contract Homes for Investors *(also available in paperback)*

Going Home... Renting to Home Ownership in 10 Easy Steps *(also available in paperback)*

In Children's Fiction:

Scary Elephant Meets the Closet Monster

In Children's Non-Fiction:

My Name is Blue: The Story of a Rescue Dog

More titles will be available in print in late 2013 and in 2014. For a current list of available print books visit:

www.ifandorbutpublishing.com

or

Amazon.com/Author/MichaelDelaware

If you found this book on real estate useful, you might also like these other titles by the same author:

Understanding

LAND

CONTRACT

HOMES

In Pursuit of the American Dream

First Party.

Second Party.

Michael Delaware

www.ingramcontent.com/pod-product-compliance
Lightning Source LLC
Chambersburg PA
CBHW022037190326
41520CB00008B/617